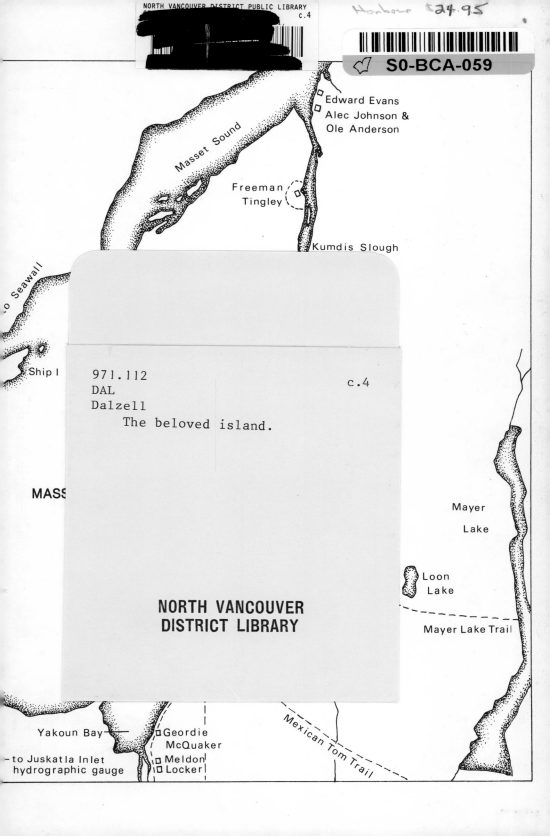

Harbour $24.95

Edward Evans
Alec Johnson &
Ole Anderson

Masset Sound

Freeman
Tingley

Kumdis Slough

o Seawall

Ship I

MASS

Mayer
Lake

Loon
Lake

Mayer Lake Trail

Yakoun Bay

Geordie
McQuaker

to Juskatla Inlet
hydrographic gauge

Meldon
Locker

Mexican Tom Trail

THE QUEEN CHARLOTTE ISLANDS
The Beloved Island

The
QUEEN CHARLOTTE ISLANDS

Volume 3

The Beloved Island

Kathleen E. Dalzell

HARBOUR PUBLISHING

Harbour Publishing Co. Ltd.
PO Box 219
Madeira Park, BC   V0N 2H0

Cover design by Roger Handling

Canadian Cataloguing in Publication Data

Dalzell, Kathleen E., 1919-
   The Queen Charlotte Islands

   Includes indexes.
   Vol. 2 first published: Cove Press, 1973.
   Partial contents:
      v. 2 Places and names—v. 3.
The beloved island
   ISBN 1-55017-011-2 (v. 2).—ISBN
1-55017-008-2 (v. 3)

   1. Names, Geographical - British Columbia -
Queen Charlotte Islands.   2. Queen Charlotte
Islands (B.C.) - History.   3. Queen Charlotte
Islands (B.C.) - Description and travel.
4. Queen Charlotte Islands - Biography.
I. Title.
FC3845.Q3D34 1989   971.1'31   C89-091334-X
F1089.Q3D34 1989

Printed and bound in Canada

ACKNOWLEDGEMENTS

MANY THANKS to my cousins, Isobel Thomas and Joan Taylor of Swansea, Wales, and Graham and Mary Thomas of Reading, England, for their hospitality and help during my trips to Britain to search out family background. I am equally appreciative of correspondingly valuable assistance given by cousin Gwyneth Lewis and Uncle Graham Williams, also of Swansea, but regret that my thanks to them are now posthumous. These far-off relations provided so many items of information and old family photos it made my research infinitely more productive.

Thanks also to my sister, Nancy Orr, and brother, John Williams, for recalling many incidents and filling in details of long-ago happenings.

My appreciation to Marie Baird, Mary Gibbs and Rick Dykun for their editing suggestions and advice, which has been most helpful as the manuscript was made ready for printing.

Lastly, but most importantly, I am indebted to my husband, Albert, who encouraged me to write this story, and who read the manuscript with a critical eye as it was put together.

—Kathleen E. "Betty" Dalzell

FOREWORD

AU HAADE, the Haida, had an elaborate and well-functioning society long before the first Europeans arrived on what is now known as the Queen Charlotte Islands. Representing the elite of Indian tribes, these master seamen roamed at will in their huge canoes. Only people with such skill could have made their homeland on the group of islands separated from the mainland coast by one of the most tempestuous seas in the world.

It takes a special adaptability to live successfully in such an environment and those who do not have this temperament do not long survive. The Charlottes have a way of weeding out the unsuitable in short order. As people from other countries "discovered" these Islands, most left quickly. But every so often there would be an adventurer who fell in love with the Islands as deeply as any of the *Au Haade*, and for this kindred soul there could never be anywhere else in the world so dear.

What sort of person feels this compulsion to live in such an isolated area? Non-Haidas come from all walks, creeds, and complexions. There is a little of the eccentric in each of them and a fierce love of independence. They thrive and find fulfillment in the challenge of their chosen home.

This book is the story of one man who came almost on an impulse and, like many others, only intended to stay a few months. In 1908 he was in his twenty-eighth year and had seen a fair amount of the world looking for just the right location. During a temporary stay in Vancouver, British Columbia, he met two experienced prospectors anxious to try the Masset Inlet area of the Queen Charlotte Islands. They took this greenhorn in hand and he had his first taste of life in the evergreen-scented forests of Graham Island. After three months of unsuccessful searching for minerals, his companions left, but the greenhorn knew he had found his place. He would stay for the rest of his life.

The adventuresome pioneer years were exhilarating and life was beginning to take on promise when World War One exploded. The reader is taken into the trenches of France via the field diary of this homesteader-turned-soldier as he joined with his neighbours to do his share in the conflict.

After the war, those who survived found a greatly altered homeland. The hard-won homesteads lay abandoned and several small settlements had disappeared completely. Too many of the men had died on the battlefields, and those who were spared were so utterly drained in body and spirit that only the most dedicated were able to summon the energy to journey back to the isolated Queen Charlotte Islands.

But for those whom there was no place on earth they would rather be—no journey *could* be too far. The Islands were home and gradually they would rebuild their lives to fit the changed circumstances.

ONE

THE SEA WAS ALIVE with great streamers of flying spume and towering white caps as the vicious cross-winds and rip-tides fought with the heaving ground swells of Hecate Strait. Wallowing in this witches brew, the *Henriette* laboriously inched eastward on her regular run from the Queen Charlotte Islands to Prince Rupert. It was March 10, 1910.

Captain Buckholtz passed one of his passengers as he struggled along the slanting deck to the bridge.

"Och! Damned old Hecate," Buckholtz shouted. "She's a real bitch today...!" The end of his sentence was lost as the wind flung the words out into the wild waters. The passenger, twenty-nine-year-old Trevor Williams, grinned in reply and pulled his collar higher against the piercing chill of the gale. Fighting to keep his footing as the ship lurched in the storm, Trevor wound one arm around a stanchion and braced himself hard against a cabin wall. The weather was terrible—no doubt about that. Nothing but snow and gales ever since the ship had left Massett six days earlier. Continually buffeted by high winds, it had taken the *Henriette* almost a week to finish servicing the rest of the settlements on the Charlottes before turning eastward for this trip across the threatening Hecate

Strait to Prince Rupert.

But it would take more than the bad temper of Hecate Strait to dampen Trevor's growing feeling of exhilaration, and he watched with pulse quickening as the waves smashed against the ship's plunging prow. He was on the last lap of a long journey. It was done now, though. He had found his Shangri-la. And, at this moment, on another equally stormy sea, his beloved Meta was crossing the Atlantic on her way to British Columbia to marry him. He still couldn't quite believe it was actually happening.

He certainly hadn't made the fortune he hoped for. Probably never would. Well...hell...that idea was only to impress the ambitious Mrs. Sam Taylor anyhow. She had never made any secret of her disapproval of his romance with Meta.

"My Meta," he said softly to himself. How was she going to adapt to life in a log cabin? With that houseful of servants in the Taylor home she'd had no opportunity to learn much in the way of housekeeping skills. But as far as that went...what the devil had he known about building a log cabin in the wilderness? Or even trying to live in the wilds? No one could possibly have been greener. Now that he had tasted it, though, he knew there could never be anywhere else for him. It was the end of a ten year search for exactly the right place.

He could hardly wait to show it all to Meta. "And you, damned old Hecate," he muttered to the seething waters, "you'd best show some manners."

The mainland shore could be seen dimly now, but it would be hours before the *Henriette* would finally reach her tie-up spot at the dock in Prince Rupert. Trevor, with memories of earlier years flooding in, gave himself up to reliving the events which had led up to this moment.

He recalled vividly the first time he'd seen Meta. Couldn't have been more than fifteen, either of them. The old Walter Road Congregational Church in Swansea...sitting with his brothers, Gwilym and Harold, chafing as usual at the compulsory attendance demanded by his parents. Church life was too important to their devout mother to permit any excuses. Must have been when Samuel Taylor had moved his expanding family to live at Brunswick Place, around the corner from Walter Road. He remembered how a shaft of sunlight coming through an upper window settled like a spotlight on Meta's fair head as she preceded her younger sister, Freda, down the aisle. Less than five feet tall and walking erectly, Meta held her head high—looking neither to the left nor the right—in contrast to Freda who was trying to take in the entire church with her glances along each line of pews. Then, as they were about to sit down, Meta suddenly glanced back, and her large brown eyes accidentally met his. The sudden surge of warmth which enveloped him was inexplicable to young Trevor.

"That's Meta Taylor and her sister," a girl in front of him had whispered to a seat-mate.

"Meta. That's an odd name," he thought.

Before long Meta, Freda, Trevor, and his brothers were all part of the large crowd of young people in the mid-Swansea area who swam and picnicked along the magnificent beaches of south Wales, then later danced in Swansea's halls the waltzes and polkas of that era. It was always the diminutive Meta who captured Trevor's interest, but his competition was formidable. There seemed to be a constant swarm of admirers around her.

He savoured other recollections from those teen years of the mid-1890s. The fiercely contested sports...Harold, his younger brother, was especially keen—always practicing running and jumping. The Williams house seemed to be full of clocks the boys had won in sports. Funny how it was usually a clock given as a prize. Then there were the long bicycle expeditions and training sessions in the 3rd Glamorgan Volunteer Brigade most of the boys belonged to. They were a smart-looking lot turned out in grey uniforms, natty white belts, and spats. Bertie Perkins was one of the leaders— Trevor's cousin, Alice Sandbrook, would later marry Bertie.

It was on one of the Brigade's camping trips to Devon that Trevor first met Hart Jenkins, who subsequently became a great pal. Hart intended to make a career of soldiering and studied all aspects of Brigade training with a zeal far outshining the rest of the boys. He became an absolute whiz in Morse signalling, remembered Trevor with admiration.

Then almost abruptly, so it seemed, it was over. They all graduated from Swansea's ancient Bishop Gore Grammar School, and it was time to get on with the future.

Watching the constant stream of ships from every country coming in and out of the sprawling Swansea docks, Trevor longed to see more of the world. But a seafaring life didn't really interest him. For one thing, you couldn't take a wife along. A civil engineer—now that's the ticket, he thought. It would offer plenty of opportunities to see far-off countries and provide the sort of income and life he could ask Meta to share.

Meta Taylor–1902. There could never be any other girl for Trevor.

Trevor L. Williams–1902. His competition was so formidable, he was afraid he would never have a chance.

TWO

MORGAN WILLIAMS, TREVOR'S father, was a big, strapping man from a long line of Welsh tenant sheep-farmers at Gadlys Farm, parish of Llandyfadwg, near Bridgend in mid-south Wales. His ancestors had worked the green valley and hills of Gadlys for generations, extending back to the reign of Henry VIII. In fact the name Gadlys was believed to come from a battle in the area during that era. As a rule it would be the oldest son of each successive Williams who would take over from the father before him. Morgan, being the seventh child in a family of twelve brothers and sisters, had little likelihood of fulfilling a significant role at Gadlys. Instead, his destiny was settled before his fifteenth birthday when there was an opportunity for him to apprentice to Thomas Hughes, the draper in Bridgend.

The indenture completed, Morgan left the lush hills and countryside of his youth for the coastal town of Swansea to put his new trade into practice. He opened a small wholesale drapers shop on Temple Street, struggling constantly to make ends meet. Ben Evans, a well-known Swansea merchant next door to Morgan's store, had been eyeing both the store and the young man for some time. He offered to buy Morgan out.

Realizing that Morgan was not only knowledgeable in his trade, but also fluent in both Welsh and English, Evans asked him to stay as manager of the drapery department in the expanded Evans store. No small part of Morgan's attraction to Evans' offer was the chance to work beside Rachel Lotherington, a winsome lass who had come from Lampeter to work in the ladies dress department of Evans' store. Morgan was badly smitten.

But this robust farmer's son was also finding life within the confines of shop walls to be an increasing frustration for his freedom-loving nature. When Henry Bannerman and Sons of Manchester offered him the job of commercial traveller and agent for the wholesale drapery firm for the entire south Wales area, he was ecstatic. It was his chance to escape from the store and, with that sort of salary and commissions, he could ask the vivacious Rachel to marry him.

They were married in 1870, living first at Northampton Place. When their family grew to include six children, Morgan moved them to the three-storied house at 20 Walter Road, across the street from the church which meant so much to Rachel and which became such a trial to her sons. As the children attained adolescence Rachel had great aspirations for them. She knew from her own background the value of a good education.

Her father, Thomas Lotherington, had spent several years as a student at St. John's College, Cambridge and had in fact published a book of poems during his time there. A college chum who vacationed during the summer in Wales persuaded Thomas to accompany him to the Lampeter area in the summer of 1842. The two young men stayed at the inn in Pencarreg near Lampeter and became friendly with the Davis family on a nearby farm. Thomas fell in love with one of the younger daughters, so much so that he came back the following summer to persuade her to marry him. But when he returned home to the family estate at Tunbridge Wells in Kent, his priggish father was appalled as he listened to his eldest son's joyous news. "A Welsh peasant...you must be mad!" he roared. A violent quarrel and the classic admonition, "...never darken these doors again," fell on deaf ears, as did the threat that Thomas would be cut off without a penny instantly.

Thomas was back in Lampeter within the week to marry his sweetheart. Because of his excellent academic education he had no difficulty in obtaining a post as master in the Lampeter Grammar School (now St. David's University). Rachel, who was born the following year, was therefore exposed to the hardworking, simple life of her mother's farming family plus the intellectual enrichment of her father's background. So she was in a position to make knowledgeable judgments.

The affable Morgan Williams agreed to Rachel's urging for the best schools for their children. Gwennie, their first-born, went to the exclusive Miss Phillips' Finishing School for Young Ladies in Swansea. Gwilym, second in line, was enrolled in the posh Llandovery College. But it was taking a severe toll financially. When it was Trevor's turn a few years later, Morgan feared this third child would put an unbearable strain on the budget if a similar course was followed.

Trevor's announcement that he would really like to go into civil engineering came as an immense relief. Morgan had known Roberts, head of one of the best engineering firms in the district, for many years and had done many favours for him. Roberts had repeatedly said he surely wished there was some way he could repay Morgan. Well, now Roberts would have his chance.

But friendship and business are seldom compatible. Shrewdly evaluating his old friend's anxiousness to have his son enter the firm, Roberts saw a golden opportunity for a side bonus. He named a large sum as the advance that would be needed plus the usual fee for apprenticeship. As Morgan's jaw dropped when the large advance was mentioned, Roberts went into a long tale about a list of applicants willing to pay many times that much and waited expectantly for Morgan to take the bait. Trevor, who had gone along to the interview, sensed his father's acute dismay. "Come," he said gently, taking the older man's arm. "I've got a better idea."

Morgan was still shaking his head in disbelief at Roberts' action as they walked out of the office. "The Swansea Technical School," said Trevor. "Not the same sort of training as this place—but it won't cost that kind of money either. And I hear old Davies is a cracker-jack instructor."

Mr. Davies proved to be every bit as good as his reputation. The students received a thorough grounding in their chosen profession, going out on extensive field trips to all the surrounding collieries. For the impatient Trevor, however, the training seemed endless. He passed his nineteenth birthday and was increasingly uncomfortable about being still dependent on his father. It was the summer of 1899.

Opportunities such as Trevor longed for seemed non-existent in Britain, but it was rumoured that if a young man could get out to one of the colonies or, in fact, almost anywhere abroad, there were plenty of chances to work into something worthwhile in a very few years.

On October 11, 1899, the Boer War broke out in South Africa, and the British Government cried out for recruits. Gwilym, now twenty-four, came home with the news that both he and Hart Jenkins were going to enlist. As the two discussed the venture, some of their fervor brushed off on Trevor. He had little interest in the propriety of the war— some row over a gold field in the Transvaal, it seemed. But it might provide just the opportunity he needed to try his luck in a new country.

Rachel and Morgan reluctantly agreed to accept his change of plans. But when Harold, now seventeen, pleaded to be allowed to go with the older boys, the answer was a firm "no."

Deciding to enlist was one thing. Accomplishing it was much more difficult. Gwilym, Trevor, and Hart had chosen the Yeomanry. To have their applications even considered they had to prove they were expert horsemen. Gwilym and Trevor had ridden the farm horses at Gadlys during visits to the Williams' grandparents, but this was not adequate to pass the tests. So, pooling funds, the three young men enrolled at a London riding school for a crash course.

Trevor chuckled silently at memories of the mishaps during that course. . .particularly the lesson requiring them to ride with crossed stirrups, a seemingly impossible feat. It was too much for Hart. "You fellows can have your Yeomanry," he told them. "I'm off to join the Infantry. I'll never get to South

January 1900. Private Trevor L. Williams, age nineteen, of the Denbighshire Hussars, 29th Company, Imperial Yeomanry, South Africa.

Lieutenant Gwilym T. Williams, Glamorgan Yeomanry, South Africa. 1902.

Shortly before the war ended, the soldiers were given an option to sign up for two additional years service. Both Hart Jenkins and Gwilym decided to do this, and were promoted to lieutenants. Trevor, however, had had enough of Africa and came home—still a private. The other two were discharged only a few months later, as it turned out.

1872—Rachel and Morgan Williams with their first-born, Gwennie. Six more children would subsequently be born to them: Gwilym, Carrie, Trevor, Harold, Gladys and Graham.

Troed-y-Bryn, the Welsh equivalent of "foot-of-the-mountain," was the name Rachel Williams chose for their home near the intersetion of De la Beche Street and Mount Pleasant in Swansea, South Wales. This photo was taken in 1987.

Harold E. Williams, who was only seventeen in 1900, was given a firm "no" when he begged to go along with Gwilym and Trevor to South Africa. This photo taken in 1912 shows him in the uniform of the Indian Police of Madras, where he spent many years.

Hart Jenkins, a boyhood chum of both Trevor and Gwilym Williams. This photo was taken in 1902. Hart would lose his life July 1, 1916 in the Battle of the Somme.

Africa with horses in a lifetime of trying." His background in the Glamorgan Brigade would serve him well in the Infantry, however.

Gwilym and Trevor persisted with the riding lessons and eventually felt their horsemanship was proficient enough to have another try at their preferred recruiting offices. Turned down by two, Trevor was finally accepted into the Denbigh-shire Hussars, 29th Company, Imperial Yeomanry, and Gwilym subsequently made the grade with the Glamorgan Yeommanry.

Early in the spring of 1900 Private Trevor Williams was sent to South Africa to fight the Boers—elated to have his great adventure under way.

THREE

THE 6,000-mile voyage from Southampton to Cape Town took twenty-seven days through rough seas the entire way. Their ship was an iron vessel, and all decks were packed solidly with troopers, supplies, and some fifty or more horses. So great was the fear of fire, the young soldiers were forbidden to use shovels to dung out after the horses in case a spark might be created. Instead, they were told to use bare hands and baskets for this task.

The journey became a nightmare.

Sea-sick horses were confined below deck with no exercise, strapped with belly-straps to keep them from falling and breaking a leg in the violently plunging ship. They were tended by the even sicker recruits who had to clean up the manure every morning and care for their animals. Each day the air became more putrid with the stench of animals and humans. One of the officers was to tell Gwilym years later that he never thought Trevor would survive the distance. "He would bring up a basket of dung, stagger to the rail and dump it, then lose his entire insides immediately after. Looked like a skeleton by the time we landed at Cape Town."

The boat did make four stops en route for coal and water—

at the Azores, Madeiras, Canary Islands, and Cape Verdes—
but the soldiers were only permitted to go ashore at the Canary
Islands. The men were mystified when they were not even
allowed contact with the boatloads of peddlers who came out
to greet them at the other stops. Instead, the natives were
violently pelted with lumps of coal by the ship's crew and
yelled at to "go away," to the intense disappointment of the
passengers. The fresh fruit obtained during the Canary Islands
stopover seemed pure nectar after the monotonous shipboard
rations and the soldiers longed for more.

Finally arriving at Cape Town, the boat was unloaded, and
troops and horses began the trek to the battleground in the
interior country. The first night out they were ordered to set
up camp in an open field. Tents were erected and guyed, and
horses were tethered in a row at the rear of the tents. Some of
the leads were tied to convenient guy ropes of a nearby tent or
two by soldiers too weary to look elsewhere. Sentries were
posted, some to care for the horses and others to watch for the
dreaded Boer Commandos whose lightning raids on other
British camps had taken a bloody toll. Exhausted, the
remaining soldiers went to bed. With ten men to a tent, plus
all their gear, it was a tight squeeze.

Trevor was dozing off when he heard one of the sentries
call, "Halt . . .! Who goes there?" He recognized the voice of
one of the experienced British Marines. That was no green
rookie suddenly spooked. His blood seemed to congeal. Was it
the commandos already?

There was no answer to the sentry's challenge. Again it
came, "Who is it?" And still no answer.

"Oh, my God!" thought Trevor, "Who in hell is it?"

"Halt or I'll shoot," called the sentry, and almost immediately a rifle shot resounded through the camp. With this, total
chaos broke loose. Absolute pandemonium and confusion.
Tents went end for end, troopers and gear tumbled this way
and that, arms and legs tangled, horses reared frantically, eyes
wild with fear . . .

It turned out that the camp had been pitched across a
regularly-used ostrich path on the outskirts of an ostrich farm.
Some of the giant birds were returning along their familiar

path in the dark. With their wits scared out of them by the shot, they panicked, charging directly into the tents, getting long legs entangled in the guy ropes. As the ostriches flailed and tents collapsed, the terror-stricken horses broke their tethers, many of them bolting along the plains dragging ropes and pieces of canvas. The hapless soldiers trying to get to their feet in the midst of all this added to the disarray and muddle.

Yes, mused Trevor, he could laugh about it now, but it was a frightening experience when it happened. Must have been days before they eventually rounded up all the horses again.

The entire Boer War was a succession of bad memories. He would never forget the first time he saw men killed in cold blood. One of the Boer groups they had engaged hoisted a white flag, then when the Britishers went forward to accept the expected surrender, other concealed Boers opened fire and killed the entire group. After this happened a second time the British commander decided on retaliation. He ordered the few Boers who had been captured earlier to be brought before him, tied to a pole, and shot. Nineteen-year-old Trevor became acutely aware of the ugliness of war.

Although the incident was perhaps justice of a sort, the general witlessness of the British leaders in their conduct of the African campaign against the wily native Boer was often incredible. Intelligence reports which were usually out of date and incorrect only added to the blunders. The morale of the soldiers was bad, and desertions were almost a daily occurrence. The carnage in horses was appalling. Imported horses could not tolerate the coarse grazing material of the African veldt, so there was no food for them except for the small amount of oats the troops could carry, yet they were expected to ride to the full each day. Small wonder that the life expectancy of the British horses was less than a month.

When eventually they were able to acquire some of the native South African horses, it made a world of difference. Even so, many of the Britishers looked down on the African horses. They could not trot and canter like the English steeds but took off on the gallop at every excuse. Trevor loved them. The wild, free gait was much more to his taste, and better still, when you had a South African horse, you knew he could look after himself when it came to foraging.

A continuing problem was the scarcity of water. Even to secure drinking water was a major undertaking, and baths were non-existent for the troops in the field. Months on end went by without any sort of washing to speak of. Trevor could still relish the time he first came on a small stream. He was on a patrol in the mountainous country near the Natal border, and the rivulet was perhaps three inches deep. In a flash he stripped off his clothes and lay full-length on the gravel bottom, savouring the exquisite luxury of water running over him and scrubbing clean at last, even if it meant using handfuls of sand and gravel to do the job.

Trevor also remembered that it was in South Africa he had one of the worst belly-aches of his life. Gad...it was horrendous! He had been sent to a farming area to search out stray Boers, mainly to confiscate their weapons to prevent sniping at British troops. Riding into the backyard of one farm, he saw a lady in the process of taking a batch of bread from an outdoor oven. The aroma was pure ambrosia to a man who had subsisted on tasteless hardtack for over a year.

He began searching through his pockets for a few shillings to purchase a loaf when he noticed the woman watching him was in a great state of alarm—obviously afraid of being attacked or raped. When he finally made her understand what he really wanted, she almost fainted with relief and shoved several loaves into his arms.

That fresh bread was absolutely delicious. He broke great hunks off, stuffing them into his mouth as he rode along. In less than an hour he consumed almost all of it. "Made a damned pig of myself," he recalled.

Then came the indigestion. It was overwhelming. He thought he would die, the pain was so excruciating. No way could he get any relief. Finally, staggering from his horse at the top of a hill, in his agony he fell face down on the steep slope and lay heels in the air. At last, in this unnatural, incongruous position he seemed to obtain some easing of the terrible pain. The memory of the experience was so lasting that for the rest of his life even the smell of freshly-baked bread would bring on feelings of revulsion.

Despite the incredible incompetence of the British High Command at the beginning of the war, it eventually emerged as a more efficient organization when the esteemed Horatio Kitchener was put in charge of the entire African campaign. By March of 1902 victory seemed pretty well assured, and on May 31, 1902, peace was declared.

During the two years of his stay Trevor had seen most of the southern part of Africa, from Johannesburg, Bloemfountain, and Pretoria to Cape Town. A beautiful country, but the class system was even more stifling than in Britain. The plight of the blacks, especially in the towns, was incredible. He had passed his twentieth and twenty-first birthdays in this land, but it was not a country he wanted to spend the rest of his life in.

Mail service during the war had been chancy at best. News from Wales had been meagre. Letters from home, especially from Meta, had been a rarity. Trevor decided to get back to Britain as fast as he could to see how things were before making serious plans for the future.

FOUR

WHEN TREVOR AND GWILYM arrived home in Swansea after the African campaign, it seemed strange not to go to the old Walter Road home of their boyhood years. But shortly after the two brothers had left for South Africa their parents had bought a picturesque house at the foot of Mount Pleasant Road, near the corner of De La Beche street. It was Morgan's pride and joy. "You choose a name for it," he said to Rachel.

With fond memories of the comfortable cottage in Pencarreg where she had lived as a girl, and which had been called Troed-y-Rhui (Foot-of-the-Hill), Rachel chose a similar name for this Mount Pleasant home in Swansea. "Troed-y-Bryn," she replied quickly, using the Welsh equivalent of "Foot-of-the-Mountain." So Morgan had a small plaque inscribed for the gate using the Welsh name.

There were other changes too. The Taylor family no longer lived in their Brunswick Place house. Instead, Samuel Taylor had moved his brood to a large home on Caswell Road in nearby Mumbles. Mrs. Taylor named it "Strathmore."

"Nice place," Morgan told Trevor. "...on a hill overlooking Langland Bay...big windows all across the front. Mr. Taylor still has his accountancy business on St. Mary's Street here—in Swansea—and commutes each day on the Mumbles train. Doing well in the office, I understand, and has taken his son, Jack, in to learn the business. Oh, by the way," he added, "we hear Meta is not at home now . . . gone off to university at Aberystwyth."

Aberystwyth lay a good seventy miles to the north and west of Swansea. Nevertheless, Trevor pumped up the tires of his bicycle and prepared to set off. In reply to his father's questioning gaze, he said simply, "I've got to see her." His muscles were strong after the rigours of South Africa, and the thought of Meta lent wondrous impetus to the venture. The seventy or more miles were pedalled with relative ease. Reaching the university he was wondering how to find her when he noticed a group of young people talking animatedly on one of the paths. The slight figure near the centre was all too familiar. She was prettier than ever.

This was the moment he had dreamed of for two years, but instead of making his presence known, Trevor was uncharacteristically overcome by self-doubt and shyness. The group of students surrounding her were all very smartly dressed and were all (or so it seemed to Trevor) clamouring for her attention. "Oh migawd," he thought, "nothing but bloody doctors, lawyers, and lord-knows-who. And me . . . a raggedy-ass private on an old bike." With all those university swells hanging about he wouldn't have a ghost of a chance. Thank heaven she hadn't seen him. What was the matter with his brains anyhow? Should have had more sense than to ride up here like this. He dodged back to where he had left the bicycle, jumped on, and peddled the over seventy miles home to Swansea, overnighting on the way. His depression was intense.

Gwilym was waiting as he hung up his coat in the hall at Troed-y-Bryn and appeared not to notice the glum face. "Thank heavens you're back, Trevor," he said excitedly. "I've got a line on a job possibility which might be just your dish. Arthur Andrews and his brother are after me to go into the office of their brokerage firm here, but I've got a chance to get into Lloyds Bank at Diss, up in Norfolk, and it's what I really want. So I suggested you. Arthur was quite interested and says

The Taylor home, "Strathmore," at the corner of Caswell Road and Southward Lane, in Mumbles, overlooking Langland Bay in the Swansea area. This is the way Strathmore looked when Samuel Taylor first purchased it. Later additions and renovations changed its appearance. In 1987 it was sold to owners who converted it to a nursing home.

Samuel Taylor and his second wife, Mary (Molly), who had great plans for all her girls, the two born to them as well as the three from Samuel's first marriage.

Molly Taylor and her daughters, Meta, reading, Marjorie by the window, Muriel at the piano and Freda, reading, facing camera. A fifth daughter, Beryl, much younger, is out of the photo.

Trevor, seated second from left, beside man with blurred head, played with the Le Havre rugby team during his time in the brokerage office of Monsieur Le Taconet in that city. This photo of the team was taken prior to a championship game in Paris. Trevor suffered a split scalp during this game, which required several stitches.

to come in and see him right away. He's a decent sort...I knew him well in school. Why don't you give it a try?"

"To get ahead with us you'll need good conversational French," Arthur Andrews told twenty-one-year-old Trevor. "The best way to get this is to go to France, live with a French family, and speak it the way they do. We happen to have an opening with Monsieur Taconet in our Le Havre office right now for a clerk. If you could take a crash course in shorthand and typing I'll put a word in for you—if you are willing." Willing! Trevor would have gone as a dustman, never mind a clerk—anything to get out of Britain at that moment.

The six-week crash course suggested by Arthur Andrews gave him a working knowledge of shorthand and two-fingered typing, then he was on his way to Le Havre. In the good-natured bantering of the lively French family where he found lodgings he was not long in bringing his grammar-school French up to a fair degree of polish. Still keenly interested in sports, he joined the energetic Le Havre rugby team which took part in games all over France.

It was a pretty good life, but the clerking job in the brokerage firm seemed to be a tediously dull occupation with little in the future for donkey's years. He was bored to tears. So when he heard of an opening at Le Touquet, a pleasure resort in the north of France, he decided "What the heck..." and sent in an application.

Sir Henry Curtis, an English millionaire, had bought land at Le Touquet fronting a wide sandy beach and was laying out a resort. Trevor found it a fine place to work—much better than the brokerage firm. But the pay was too meagre for a man trying to fill Samuel Taylor's financial shoes so he could court his daughter—and Trevor still nursed this dream despite everything his common sense told him.

He had been in France for about two years by this time, and among the friends he'd made was an extremely clever German who spoke several languages. This was Gunter, owner of a thriving import-export business in France. Gunter wanted to open a branch office in the Argentine but needed someone with office experience who could also speak fluent English and French to take charge. He put a proposition to Trevor.

Would he take on the job?

The challenge was irresistible. And the pay was especially attractive. "Just give me time for a visit home to Wales, then I'll meet you in Buenos Aires whenever you say," Trevor told him.

Although it was one of the prime reasons he wanted to return to Swansea at that time, Trevor could not muster the courage to visit the Taylor home to see Meta. Better find out the lay of the situation first. He got in touch with Jack, the elder of Meta's two brothers. Over a pint in a pub, he was not long in coming to the point.

"She's gone to Cornwall," Jack Taylor said in answer to his supposedly casual query.

"Cornwall!" exclaimed Trevor, fearing the worst.

"Yes, Father sent her down to set up books for one of his clients."

"Good Lord! I thought she would have been married . . . or at least planning to by now," Trevor said, unable to disguise his relief.

"Well, that's part of the problem," Jack told him. "Mother keeps on at her to marry one of these fellows who keep coming to call and Meta won't give any of them a tumble. They've had some fearful rows. Father badly needed someone he could trust to do the accounts for a few of his clients outside Swansea. He and I have more than enough to do here, even though we have increased the staff considerably. Meta really is a whiz at figures, and she wanted to get away so badly, Father agreed to let her go to Cornwall to fix up a few accounts we have there. Mother was up in arms about it, but Meta went anyhow."

Taking Trevor's arm, Jack led him to a table off to one side where they would have more privacy. "Meta will probably kill me for this," he began, "but I'm damned sure the reason she's having so many rows with Mother is because of you. She's always had a secret yen for you. Well, it's not such a secret, really. We all know it. And it's making Mother just furious . . she's got her plans all set for each of the girls. And you—you damned donkey—here you are, chasing off all over creation. It's obvious that you like Meta as much as she fancies you.

Why don't you go after her, man? You'd better get in the running before the family wears her down."

"...she's always had a secret yen for you..." Trevor felt as though his heart would burst with elation. He left for Cornwall the next morning, to the small coastal village of Looe, and took rooms at an inn near her lodgings. Each day they took long walks, talking about everything under the sun. The evenings were spent sharing dinners and dreams. The books of Samuel Taylor's client were put to one side without a single twinge of conscience by Meta. It was an idyllic two weeks.

"Just as soon as I get established in the Argentine, I'm coming to see your father about us getting married," Trevor told her. Meta longed to tell him how foolish it was to waste their lives apart while he amassed the amount of money he seemed to think necessary to impress her parents, but she knew this was not the time. Let him find his niche, then she would persuade him.

She instinctively realized that Trevor could never be happy in the set pattern of existence in Britain. He was a free soul, and the trappings of tradition and class distinction so dear to the hearts of most Britishers were not for him. It had been this very vibrancy of spirit which captivated her so many years earlier and totally spoiled her for anyone else—even though he had given her precious little encouragement to feel that she was anything more than a schoolday romance of their youth.

But now that she knew he was truly in love with her, her dream had come true. She could face all the inevitable storms at home.

FIVE

BUENOS AIRES PROVED TO BE a bustling metropolis in the summer of 1904 when Trevor arrived to set up Gunter's import office.

"It's a beautiful city," he wrote Meta, "with fine parks and squares and theatres. And the most magnificently wide streets. You should see especially the width of the Avenue of 9th of July—supposed to be the widest street in the world, and I can well believe this. It far surpasses anything I've ever laid eyes on. But I think the most attractive is Avenida del Mayo, a broad, tree-lined boulevard which runs for a mile or more between Plaza del Mayo and Plaza del Congresso, where the government meets to make the laws of this country. There is a wide variety of sports, so I'm able to get in a fair amount of football and tennis."

The little importing office operated with relative smoothness until Trevor began to realize that some of Gunter's business practices were not as ethical as they should be. Under query, Gunter was evasive. Equally unsatisfactory was his explanation regarding the lack of a paycheque for Trevor after three months of work. "Just getting organized takes time....- but the money is good...don't worry. Should have everything in order soon," was his reply.

Another month passed and Trevor's growing unease made a decision necessary. Obviously he was in a bad situation with Gunter. He'd better get out—and fast. Noting an advertisement in an evening paper for an assistant manager of a cattle ranch several hundred miles inland in the pampas region, he sent in an application. It was accepted by return mail, and the importing office was left behind with infinite relief. However, there was a not unexpected blow. Gunter, charging that Trevor had violated their contract, refused to pay a cent—no salary nor Trevor's fare from Britain which had been part of the deal. So he went to his new job with empty pockets.

The cattle ranch, Estancia La Evelina at Manantiales, was the home of La Compania de Tierras and Productos Limited. Owned by an English firm and running over ten thousand head of stock, it was a large operation for those parts, and in this exceedingly fertile pampas area it was not uncommon to get three crops a year. Trevor thoroughly enjoyed every aspect of the life. Plenty of opportunity to ride at full gallop, the way he had learned on the South African veldt.

It was on this ranch that he first encountered the Argentine gauchos, superb horsemen with a justifiable pride in their skill. They wore a distinctive type of clothing—small round hats, baggy trousers, wide belts, and colourful neck scarves. Most of them also carried a poncho which they used either as a cape or blanket.

But a gaucho was strictly a horseman and cowboy. He did not do any of the menial ranch jobs such as painting or digging fence-post holes. On this ranch the menial jobs were done by the son of a British earl. This young man so loved the experience of ranch life that his parents paid handsomely for him to stay there. "Not a bad bloke, either," Trevor wrote Meta. "At least he does know how to work when he has a mind to, and has enough sense to realize that this is a more useful mode of living than chasing foxes in England."

The paycheques were issued quarterly, and this was when Trevor received a second let-down. He had understood the salary to be the equivalent of $120 a month, but now found the $120 was for the quarter...a mere $40 a month. Even with everything found, this amount of cash would not do for the man hoping to marry Samuel Taylor's daughter. It was a bitter disappointment, for he really loved the ranch life.

The "Help Wanted" columns were listing an opening for a chief engineer's assistant for the Entre Rios Railway Company in Parana. The wages sounded excellent. His application accepted, Trevor left the ranch at Manantiales to return to Buenos Aires and board the boat which would take him up the Parana River to the job. And if he had thought the streets in this country were big—they were nothing to the size of the rivers. "I honestly thought the whole region must be in the throes of a flood," he wrote his father. "Never dreamed there could be rivers this big. Miles and miles of water."

The sternwheeler which took him upriver was an elegant vessel with staterooms and an excellent dining room where they served fine wines with meals. It took several days of travelling up the Plata, then the Parana, to reach Parana village. "And what should be anchored in mid-stream off Parana but a big, rusty old British tramp steamer," he told his father. "She was loading quebracho wood, a heavy but much-prized hardwood. The sight of this ocean-going ship so far inland almost caused me to rub my eyes in disbelief."

"The name 'quebracho' means 'axe-breaker,' one of the other passengers told Trevor. "It's an exceptionally hard wood, almost indestructible and much in demand for railroad ties. They say some sills put in the ground near here were dug up after three hundred years and found to be in perfect condition."

The Entre Rios Railroad Company of Parana was under British ownership and management, with about ninety men on the payroll when Trevor arrived. He had picked up a smattering of Spanish in Buenos Aires and on the ranch. Finding lodgings with a Spanish family in Parana and using that language almost exclusively, he soon became adept at making himself understood.

The railroad company had ordered several big Baldwin locomotives from Britain, and the Baldwin manufacturers sent a Mr. R.J. Waters to Parana to instruct the Entre Rios personnel in the maintenance and care of the big engines.

Waters was an expert at his job but, lacking any knowledge of Spanish, was unable to tell the workmen what he wanted done. He talked about his dilemma to Trevor.

"The only way to learn that type of Spanish is to live with a Spanish-speaking family," Trevor advised. "I'll see if the family I lodge with will take on another newcomer, and perhaps I'll be able to give you a hand with the basics of the language until you get the feel of it." Waters agreed and the two men formed a strong friendship. (Some years later this same Waters was to act as best man for Meta and Trevor at their wedding on the west coast of British Columbia.)

The chief engineer for the Entre Rios Railroad, J.A. Carrod, had been with the firm for years and knew the ways of the company and the country inside out. He was a fairly easy man to work with, as Trevor discovered when he became Carrod's assistant. Until one day. Trevor had to sign each of the ninety or more paycheques every week—a task which gave him an acute case of writer's cramp and bit into his time considerably. As it was such a routine procedure, he had a rubber stamp made and breezed through the operation with ease. When the Chief heard about his innovation he was appalled and threatened to fire him on the spot. Trevor was equally adamant. It was stupid to waste all his time writing his name over and over again, he argued. The rubber stamp was the obvious answer.

News of the row reached the company manager, Follett Hunt, who sent for Trevor. "You are a darned good man, Williams," he said. "I don't want to lose you over such a trifling matter. Let's see if we can't work something out."

In the course of their discussion Trevor said how much he liked working for the company—pay was excellent and so on. "I'm thinking of getting married and bringing my wife out to live here," he said. Hunt appeared to be electrified by this statement. Jumping up from his chair he came round to the front of his desk—visibly concerned.

"Oh, my boy," he began earnestly. "Don't even consider such a thing. Not ever! This is no place for a woman who has lived all her life in Britain. They simply cannot stand the climate. Look at me. Married for over twenty years. I never see my family to speak of. My wife has to live in England for most of the year. Both my sons go to school in England. It's a terrible way to live. But it's the same with all northern European women. They just can't exist in this climate—seems to sap every ounce of their strength. Take my advice, Williams, don't bring a British girl out here. Not if you want any kind of a normal life. It just won't work. Better take up with one of the locals."

Trevor walked dejectedly back to his lodgings. The fuss with old Carrod could be settled—no real problem there. But this news about English women not being able to stand the climate—that was a shocker. He'd never heard of this before. Damn! It was a hell of a good job with excellent prospects for the future. He liked the fellows he worked with and the free and easy way of the country. But what the devil use was it if he couldn't have Meta here to share it? And he wanted no part of the life Follett Hunt had just described.

Waters listened carefully as Trevor told him about the interview. "He was so sincere I have to take what he said very seriously," Trevor explained. "And come to think of it, none of our staff here do have British wives. Anyone with a so-called proper home is married to a local woman," he sighed. "I really don't know what to do. Guess I should have figured it was all too good to be true—there was bound to be some bloody thing happen. But I never thought of this."

The two men sat in silence for several minutes, then Waters spoke, "I'm hoping to go to Canada after this job—I know a few of the chaps from the Baldwin firm who went out there with some of our engines, and they just raved about the country. Might be just the place for you, too, Williams...not too much spit and polish. Should be plenty of opportunities for a fellow with your qualifications—certainly as many as there are down here."

As Waters enthusiastically described his idea of Canada, Trevor's interest was whetted. However, he was hard put to overcome his disappointment. It had been nearly two years since he had come to the Argentine, and now to realize that it would have to be still longer before he could ask Meta to join him was hard to accept. Well, before he went chasing off to a new country he was going home to see her.

Not wanting to waste any of his newly-acquired bank account on a trans-Atlantic fare, he got a job on a cattle-boat and worked his passage to Britain. He would use some of the money saved by this to indulge in a splash when he got to Swansea. Landing in Liverpool several weeks later, he telegraphed his family that he would be arriving at the train depot in Swansea the following day.

There was much rejoicing in the Williams' home, and two younger brothers, Harold and Graham, volunteered to meet him. Harold, then twenty-three, was home on leave from service with the Madras Police in India, and Graham, the youngest of the family, had recently passed his eighteenth birthday and had just returned from an excursion to France and Spain.

"Father had given us such glowing reports of Trevor in the Argentine," Graham said later, "that both Harold and I felt we had to dress to the nines for the occasion. Harold, always a very smart dresser, got decked out in a beautiful brown suit with a chic peach tie and collaborated trimmings, and I did my best with my newly-purchased continental finery.

"We naturally looked in the first-class section for our glamorous brother from South America. No sign. Well, perhaps he would be in the second-class seats. . . although we could hardly believe he would come home in that type of accommodation. Still no sign.

"Just as we were about to give up, from the back of the train came a somewhat dirty-looking gent with a rag around his throat and a 'gorblimey' cap, grinning hugely at our obvious disconcertion. 'Oh, good God,' said Harold. 'Don't tell me we have to walk up through the town with something like *that*!' But Trevor caught up with us too quickly for any change of plans. He didn't need to tell us he had worked his way home on a cattle-boat. He looked and smelled the part all too plainly."

SIX

THE FOUR-WEEK VISIT WITH his family and Meta passed far too quickly, but Trevor, anxious to find out what the opportunities were in Canada, sailed for Montreal in the fall of 1906. He was now twenty-six years old. Fluent in both English and French, and with references to support his statement of office experience, he found work in this bustling, predominately French-speaking city within a few days. The new job was as an assistant to the purchasing agent for the Canadian White Company, a large engineering firm with headquarters in the United States. It would do while he had a look around and got his bearings.

He found it a congenial firm and soon made a number of friends among the employees. Joe and Harry Weare became his special pals, and Harry invited him to spend his first Canadian Christmas with their family in the Westmount district of Montreal. Joe took him skating. Trevor chuckled as he recalled his awkwardness for the first few times on skates. H.A. Cassil, the purchasing agent, introduced him to tobogganing and snowshoeing, and of all the winter sports it was the snowshoeing he enjoyed most.

In the summer the young men went on trips to nearby

Cartierville and St. Rose to fish and hike. And although Trevor hadn't intended to remain in the Montreal area when he first arrived, he decided to stay on at least until the winter of 1907, then make up his mind. It was a pleasant existence, so his indecision was puzzling. However, there was something inexplicable causing him to want to reserve judgment for a few months.

His intuition served him well. For with the winter of 1907 there came a year of great financial panic. Businesses, banks, railroad companies, and many others went into receivership in the United States as well as Canada. The Canadian White Company was among those caught in the crash, and in March, 1908, they closed their doors for good.

It appeared hopeless to find any sort of work. Trevor was pondering his best move when Tom, one of the men he worked with at the office, came round to his lodgings. "I think I'm getting out of Montreal as fast as I can," he told Trevor. "It's going to be a grim situation here—too many people looking for work. I've an uncle on Vancouver Island—out on the west coast of British Columbia. He runs a small market-garden business. Think I'll go and see him and perhaps find something to do. How about coming with me, Trevor? I'd like company on the trip, and it would give you a good chance to see the country."

"That sounds interesting," Trevor replied. "I'll let you know definitely in a day or two. Got a few loose ends I want to check out first."

He had become friendly with a reporter on the Montreal Gazette, William James Raymond, who seemed to have a better than average general knowledge of Canada. "What do you think of the idea, Bill?" Trevor asked. "Well, to tell the truth, Williams," Raymond answered, "I've been thinking of going west myself... in fact I have an application in right now for a job on a Saskatoon paper, but I've a hankering to go to British Columbia eventually. Who knows? Maybe we'll meet there if you stay any length of time." The description Bill Raymond gave to Trevor of Canada's west coast was all the inducement Trevor needed. He would take that trip with Tom.

Because Tom wanted to go to Toronto to visit his family for a few weeks, Trevor decided to visit New York City and Niagara Falls during that time. Then, meeting in Toronto, the two men left for British Columbia, crossing the continent by train through the United States, stopping for a few days in all the main cities en route. Everywhere they went they saw throngs of men walking the streets, hungry and desperate. It didn't seem to be a good omen. Eventually arriving in Seattle, the two travellers boarded a boat for Vancouver, British Columbia. Conditions there were not any better. They crossed to Vancouver Island, spent a few days in Victoria, then went on to Duncan where Tom found his uncle and prepared to stay for awhile.

Trevor returned to Vancouver and checked into a small hotel. A sign of the desperate times was the extremely modest price—a nice room and breakfast for only $8.00 a month. And in many of the cafes a nourishing meal could be had for fifteen cents. It was as good a place to stay as any, until he could decide on his next move.

Among the guests registered at the same hotel was an interesting man named Jack Davies. As a seasoned prospector he had many intriguing tales to tell and was particularly full of glowing accounts of a trip he had made the previous year to a group of islands in the north, the Queen Charlottes. It was the first time Trevor had ever heard of them.

"Well, there's two main islands, really," Jack explained, taking a pencil to draw a rough map on the back of an envelope. "Moresby in the south and a larger one, Graham, in the north. . . with lots of smaller ones clinging along the ends and sides. They're about four hundred miles north of Vancouver, and I would judge they lie perhaps about a hundred miles off the mainland. Rough water for those hundred miles, but. . . man are those islands ever something!"

Jack had prospected all around Moresby during the 1907 mineral rush without finding much, but he was very keen to have a look at the more northerly Graham Island. It was a chance of a copper find that lured him. "There's a big inlet. . . almost like a lake in the centre of Graham," he told Trevor, "and no one has really checked around this for

Montreal–1908. Park Toboggan Slide. Winter sports like this were a novelty for Trevor.

Of all the winter sports, it was snowshoeing that Trevor enjoyed most. This photo of him was taken early in February, 1908, when he and an office chum were on a "tramp" to Mount Royal.

Henry Edenshaw's *Josephine*, as it looked in May 1908 when Trevor Williams, Charles Copp and Jack Davies hitched a ride from Port Simpson to Masset. Later an engine was installed and the cabin remodelled extensively.

Jack Davies walks towards the tent. On land he was hard to keep up with, but in a boat he was in abject terror most of the time. This photo taken in May 1908, is of the camp they made at the mouth of the Nadu River, where they found a few "colours" when they tried panning.

minerals, although there's been a lot of good coal discovered in the Yakoun Valley, which lies to the south of this place. The inlet is called Massett Inlet," he added, pencilling the name on his map. But Jack Davies had run out of funds.

He introduced Trevor to Charlie Copp, another experienced prospector who had seen most of the mining fields in British Columbia. Copp was fired by Jack's enthusiasm to have a look at Massett Inlet and had enough cash to finance his share of the venture. Normally he would have nothing to do with greenhorns in the bush, but he sized Williams up and apparently liked what he saw. "Why don't you come with us?" he suggested to Trevor. "Grubstake Jack and yourself. We'll show you the ropes, and if we find anything we'll split it three ways."

Although somewhat skeptical of any so-called fortune to be made, Trevor was intrigued by the offer. There certainly weren't going to be many jobs around Vancouver for awhile, and in any case he'd really had enough of sitting at an office desk. Here was a chance to be initiated into bush life by two obvious professionals.

Under the guidance of his new partners, he went first to Andy Linton's to buy one of the famous Linton boats, a sixteen-foot, clinker-built, double-ender. Then to various suppliers to pick up sails, tent, collapsible stove, and grocery items to tide them over for six months. These were all loaded on board the CPR's *Amur* which left Vancouver for Skidegate on May 2, 1908. (Skidegate was the only point on Graham Island which had regular boat service at that time.)

As the *Amur* steamed north along the mainland coast of British Columbia, she put into several small places along the way to unload freight and passengers. On the morning of May 5th, she docked at the tent town of Prince Rupert, the embryo terminus for the Grand Trunk Pacific Railroad which was gradually being built westward.

"Arrived at this much-talked-about place around 9 a.m." Trevor wrote in his diary. "Raining so heavily it was hard to get a good look at the place. A few wooden buildings, many canvas ones—including P.O. and police station. Everywhere stumps and rough ground. Population said to be six hundred.

Many of these were idle and crowded the wharf as we tied up.
The Grand Trunk Pacific owns all of Kaien Island, on which
the town is situated, but so far has not sold any land. There is a
newspaper, a single sheet called *The Empire* which sells for ten
cents. Undoubtedly, this will someday be an important place.
At present it is a pioneer town in the making. There were
construction camps in the woods along the shore preparing for
the future railroad."

The *Amur* left Prince Rupert at supper time and reached
Port Simpson a few hours later. Port Simpson was the main
town on the north coast and the supply centre for many of the
outlying places. It was from here they would cross the open
water of Hecate Strait to their destination of Skidegate.

A schooner from Massett, the *Josephine*, was tied to the
dock, and Copp picked up the information that her skipper,
Henry Edenshaw, a Massett Haida Indian, had brought passengers over to catch the *Princess May*, due in Port Simpson in
a few days. Edenshaw was waiting to pick up more passengers
from the *Princess May* to go back to Massett with him. "If we
could get a lift over with him," Copp told his partners, "we'd
save that long sail from Skidegate to Massett. What say I ask
him?"

"Be a pretty tight squeeze," Edenshaw said after counting
heads and looking at the baggage, "but I think we can make
room." All the prospecting supplies would have to be
repacked and loaded into the Linton, which would be towed
behind the *Josephine*. Copp and Davies were old hands at this
sort of thing, and with Edenshaw looking on to make sure the
items were stowed in the manner to give the best balance for
efficient towing, the Linton was made ready for the journey.

"When the *Princess May* docked," Trevor entered in his
diary, "I could hardly believe my eyes. Who should I see
leaning on the rail but an old friend from the South African
campaign. A good lad, and notable for the hesitation when his
name was due to be called at mail-time or roll-
call...Prythwrch." Prythwrch was on his way to Alaska and
equally amazed to see Trevor on this side of the globe.

The *Josephine* sailed for Massett as soon as her passengers,
six white men and six Haida Indians, were rounded up and

aboard. Strong head winds forced them to anchor at Dundas Island for a few hours, but when these abated the schooner was soon out in Hecate Strait. It was a lumpy trip. But they made good time despite this and arrived at the Indian village of Massett shortly before 4 p.m. The heavily-laden Linton, being towed astern, survived the crossing in good shape.

"Friday, 8th May, 1908," Trevor began his letter to Meta. "First set foot on this most westerly part of the British Empire. From the great horn of Rose Spit at the northeastern extremity of these Queen Charlotte Islands, we sailed past a sand beach some thirty miles long to the mouth of the river-like Massett Sound. The beach reminds me of Oxwich at home. The Massett Indian village is just inside the entrance of Massett Sound, on the east shore. Carved poles positioned along the shoreline of the village are intriguing. Jack Davies says he saw similar poles in Indian villages on Moresby Island to the south of this island. They are said to depict legends and crests of the families of the Haida nation.

"Our capable skipper, Edenshaw, who apparently plies an active trade ferrying passengers from Massett to Port Simpson, is also the hotel-keeper, school-teacher, and storekeeper in Massett. We arranged to put up at his hotel for a few days as we have to obtain permission from the head man in this village, Chief Weah, to use Indian-owned camping sites.

"Our boat, piled high with supplies, was pulled above the high-tide mark in case of a storm, and during the time we were here, not a single item in the boat was disturbed. If the children, curious, would go near it, they were immediately cautioned away by their elders. I was very impressed."

Copp made the presentation of gifts to the Chief, which was customary in this situation, and in turn received the permissions needed. They could proceed. The boat was unloaded, dragged to the water's edge, refloated and reloaded, then anchored to await the start of the flood tide. There was a six-knot current in Massett Sound, so the stage of the tide was all-important. Edenshaw had told them the Sound extended south for about twenty miles before opening into the lake-like Massett Inlet, their ultimate destination.

It was getting on in the day when they left Massett, so camp was made for the first night at the mouth of Watun River, about ten miles south of Massett. Copp, taking a few sample washings with his "pan," thought he could see minute specks of gold dust in the fine sand of one washing. After more testing and scrutiny by both he and Davies, they decided to follow the river upstream the next day. However, they found nothing more and came to the conclusion it was only a freak showing.

The same thing happened at their next campsite at the mouth of the Nadu River, some five or six miles south of Watun. Diligently following this creek to its headwaters, constantly testing all the way, the prospectors decided that this too was an isolated happening. They discussed reports they had heard about fine gold dust being found in black sand areas on parts of the east coast of this Graham Island—dust so fine it was impossible to recover any paying amounts. "Likely our samples come from the same sandy sources which no doubt underlie most of the muskeg on this northeastern end," said Jack. "Not enough to go chasing after." Copp agreed.

After testing the shorelines, creeks, and valleys on both sides of Massett Sound, they slowly made their way into the expanse of Massett Inlet.

"Copp and Davies are artists in making camp," Trevor wrote his father. "I simply couldn't have had better teachers and will never regret this trip. Davies is an especially skilled woodsman and completely fearless in his ability to survive anywhere in the bush. He can carry on his back everything he needs to make a home—tarpaulin, axe, pots, flour, and dried fruit. Using material from the forest he will have a comfortable camp set up in no time at all. Boughs for beds, dinner of bannock, stewed fruit, and a few fish, clams, or perhaps a duck of some sort to round out the meal. He can hike for miles every day, and Copp and I are hard-put to keep up with him.

"But in the boat he is panic-stricken. We have an awful time with him. Most of the shorelines have to be skirted so closely on his account that the keel of the boat frequently scrapes bottom. It is a nuisance, and Copp tells him off about it pretty strongly, but nothing seems to ease his terror.

"We use the Indian camping cabins as shelters whenever we can, instead of the tent. These are light pole frames covered with bark or shakes and with one door. An open fire-pit in the centre of the room is for heat and cooking. As long as one keeps the door shut, the smoke seems to go straight up through a hole in the roof. Davies sets up the cooking arrangement on an ingeniously notched branch for the pails over the fire, and altogether we are most comfortable no matter what the weather is like outside. So far we have not seen another human soul, but I'll give this letter to Edenshaw to take to the mainland to mail when we return to Massett in a few weeks."

For three months the men rowed, sailed, or hiked all around the western and southern shores of the basin-like Massett Inlet region, stopping at each creek or river to examine the channels, climbing through the valleys and up and down most of the mountainsides, but except for some copper stain in Juskatla and the few flecks of gold at Watun and Nadu Rivers, they found nothing to warrant further prospecting. Copp and Davies decided to pack up and return to the mainland.

But for Trevor it had been the most interesting and satisfying three months of his life. He wanted more of this way of living. That soft, evergreen-scented air in a land with so much space for a man to stretch and breathe in was the Shangri-la he had subconsciously dreamed of for most of his days. If he could find some way to make a living, this would be the place he would like to stay forever. He was twenty-eight now. Most of his money was gone, but he had a good boat, tent, stove, and supplies for one man for at least six months—plus plenty of ambition. It was worth a try.

After delivering his partners to Massett to catch one of the Indian schooners sailing to Port Simpson, Trevor pitched his tent on a grassy spot near a water-hole on the south side of Delkatla Slough. It was a quiet place. His nearest neighbour was Charles Harrison, a retired Anglican minister, who lived with his wife and two sons at the head of the Slough, about a mile east of Trevor's tent.

Around the middle of July the steamer *Coquitlam* made a

special trip to the Massett area to bring in a number of passengers who settled on land on the west side of Massett Sound, opposite Delkatla Slough. Some of these hardy souls went inland as much as six miles to find a piece of property. Trevor was able to pick up quite a few jobs ferrying them back and forth across the Sound in his boat.

Later that same month a man named Francis, an ex-lighthouse keeper from one of the Great Lakes, arrived from Vancouver on a small sailing sloop and anchored in the Slough near Trevor's camp. When he heard that Trevor had been to Massett Inlet, Francis asked to be shown the way. The boat was a decked-over sailing yacht, cabin-under-deck, big mast, sails, and bowsprit, plus a fin-shaped leaded keel which drew nine feet of water. It certainly could sail. They tacked south along Massett Inlet, inside Ship Island, and around the islands on the west side of Massett Inlet. (In later years when charts were made which showed the innumerable rocks and reefs through which they had sailed, Trevor marvelled at their incredible luck with that nine-foot draft.)

Seeing smoke at the head of a bay on the east side of Massett Inlet and a fair-sized sailboat anchored close by, Francis made towards it with all sails set. He pooh-poohed Trevor's suggestion of caution. The high tide showed nothing but water up to and around their objective. But that nine-foot keel hit bottom half a mile away. They got the sails down in a rush, lucky not to have lost some of the rigging overboard, and Francis sheepishly admitted he should have used his lead line in such unknown waters.

The boat they could see safely anchored there was Eli Tingley's thirty-foot Columbia River type sloop, which had a centre-board and tall mast. However, with the centre-board up, it drew just over fifteen inches of water, not the nine feet of Francis' craft. They were soon to learn that this bay, which Tingley called Stewart Bay, was very shallow—in fact dried almost completely with each low tide. Tingley anchored his boat in a small stream which entered the head of the bay, close to his newly-built log cabin.

Going ashore to visit, Trevor and Francis received a hearty welcome from Eli, who told them he had come to this region

After obtaining permission from Chief Weah of Masset, the three prospectors were able to use the Indian cabins to camp in. This photo dated June 9, 1908, shows the inside of the Indian cabin at the Canoe Entrance to Juskatla Inlet. A welcome haven in bad weather. As long as the door was kept shut, the smoke went up through the hole in the roof designed for this.

Charles Copp rows the Linton at the mouth of the Ain River. Note Indian cabins in centre of photo. Taken June 1908.

Elias James Tingley, "Eli."

A young man with a vision of a townsite.
Photo–B.L. Tingley

the year before (1907) with two friends, Allan Stewart and Emerson Calhoun. They came from their homes in Victoria, all fired up by the British Columbia Government bulletins extolling the wonderful agricultural possibilities on Graham Island—especially the northern part. This was the first Trevor had heard about that aspect, so Eli dug some of the booklets out of a box to show him.

"Don't see how you could resist," Trevor commented as he leafed through the lavishly worded material.

"Well, I wasn't so interested in farming," Eli replied, "but we had a good friend in the Premier's office, and it was his information that Massett Inlet would be an ideal place to set up a townsite to take advantage of the big land rush. I kind of liked the idea of locating a townsite...that's why I came. I think Allan just came to see the country, but Emerson was scouting land for his family and some friends from Alberta."

Eli continued: "We came to Skidegate on the *Amur*, then hiked north along the east coast to Tlell. We knew there was a trail from Tlell to Massett Inlet and, after quite a hunt, finally picked up the succession of blazes which ran in this direction. Couldn't call it a 'trail'... but anyhow it came out right to this spot here, where I have my cabin. When we were making camp that night Allan cut his foot pretty badly. We bandaged him up, but there was no way he would be able to walk on it for awhile. So we fixed him up with wood, water, and food and left him here to heal while Emerson and I explored around."

"Went north," Eli gestured towards what he called Kumdis Slough. "Quite a bit of natural grassland along the edges of the Slough, which interested Emerson. Then about two-thirds of the way north along Kumdis Island we came upon a ranch of sorts belonging to Freeman Tingley. No relation to me," he added. "Freeman was full of the agricultural opportunities possible in this region, and Emerson was pretty impressed by what he said. We had to wait until Allan's foot healed well enough to walk, then we hiked back to Skidegate and took the *Amur* south.

"Named this bay," he pointed to the water in front of his cabin, "Stewart Bay, for Allan. He was so disappointed when he had to lay up with that cut foot while Emerson and I were tramping around."

The reports brought back to those waiting in Victoria were so promising that in the spring of 1908 a party of seventeen packed and made ready to go to the Charlottes to settle. In addition to Eli, Allan, and Emerson, there was also Bert Tingley, Eli's brother; John Calhoun, Emerson's seventy-year-old father; Emerson's brother, Jack Calhoun; his sister Anna and her husband, James Johnston, plus their five children; as well as three other Albertans, Mr. S. Peterson and his sister, Anna, and a Mr. J. Watson. As they were about to leave, Russ Rumball, a miner Allan, Eli, and Bert had known in their gold rush days of '98 in the Yukon, also decided to join the party.

"We had a huge amount of stuff," Eli told Trevor and Francis, "So we chartered the *Vadso*, but about a hundred miles from Victoria the ship hit a reef near Cape Lazo and filled with water. We managed to get our stuff off and put it ashore at Union Bay. Then a couple of us went to Vancouver to arrange for the *Amur* to pick everyone up and take the party by special charter to Massett. Locke was the skipper, and he brought us up Massett Sound to the Nadu River, even though the water is uncharted. Well...we gradually ferried everything ashore. Some job! In addition to a mountain of provisions, there was lumber and farming equipment—even horses! And we had three boats, a fourteen-footer, sixteen-footer, and this thirty-foot Columbia River boat of mine. We moved the stuff up onto Kumdis Island near Freeman Tingley's and set up a temporary camp—then everyone fanned out looking for the place they wanted."

But they were bitterly disappointed. Expecting to see the land described in government bulletins as "ready for the plough," they found instead so much timber and muskeg it would take years to make a paying farm. Even the grassland would need extensive draining. After a soul-searching conference they decided to cut their losses and abandon the project. Luckily they found a market for all their belongings at Massett—even the horses brought a good price. Then everyone left Port Simpson on two chartered Indian schooners. Everyone except Eli, who had fallen in love with the land and would remain. He was still irresistibly attracted to the idea of becoming a townsiter.

Allan and Emerson also stayed behind long enough to help Eli build his sixteen by sixteen-foot log cabin and cut a stack of firewood before they, too, left. Eli had chosen for his townsite land at the head of Stewart Bay, terminus of the blazed trail to Tlell—which he now knew was called the Mexican Tom Trail. He was currently in the process of setting out his preemption stakes to take in 160 acres on the heavily wooded point between Stewart Bay and the mouth of the Yakoun River.

"But I'm not the only one here," he told Trevor. "There's a fellow up around the corner in Kumdis Bay—about three or four miles north and east of here—George Mayer. He came in about a year ago and put up a cabin. Plans to preempt land there."

Trevor and Francis returned to Delkatla and found work as chainmen at $2.50 a day for a survey that a youthful Fred Nash, BCLS, had been engaged to do for one of the first of the North Beach land speculators, the genial A.S. Christie, a boot manufacturer from Vancouver. As everything connected with the survey had to be packed in on the crew's backs, they were limited in their camping equipment. No tent. Only a small tarpaulin to sleep under. No stove. The food was cooked over an open fire, and meals consisted invariably of beans, bacon, dried fruit, and tea. It was a far cry from the camps Trevor had enjoyed with Copp and Davies.

The job was pure misery from beginning to end. Cutting through dense, jungle-like salal, usually soaking wet, was backbreaking, and as it rained almost continuously they were drenched to the skin most of the time with no opportunity to dry their clothes. The hours were long. It was often past nine o'clock each night before they stumbled wearily along the rough trails back to camp, ate their monotonous meal, then crawled exhausted into their perpetually wet blankets. Added to these discomforts were the clouds of flies circling ceaselessly, looking for bare flesh. Even so, there was a curious satisfaction in completing the work.

Caught up in the optimism of Eli Tingley and A.S. Christie as to the future possibilities of the Graham Island area, and irresistibly attracted to the challenge of frontier life, Trevor was wrestling with some hefty decisions.

From the bulletins in Eli's cabin, he knew that being a British subject he was entitled to 160 acres of land in unsurveyed territory. He would have to live for two years on the land he staked, do $400 worth of improvements—a decent log cabin from material on one's own claim would accomplish the latter. Then when the two years were up he would have to pay the Government $1 per acre, plus $10 for a Crown Grant and assume the costs of having his land surveyed, and the land was his—free and clear. To the grandson of a Welsh tenant-farmer it sounded like the bargain of a lifetime. But what about Meta? And Samuel Taylor?

On the other hand, what was the use of going back to more populated centres? Reports indicated jobs were even scarcer now, and having had a taste of this bush life, he honestly didn't think he could go back to the four walls of an office. Well . . . damn. Why not give this a try?

The big problem was to learn what land was available. Information of sorts, all very sketchy, could be obtained from blueprints made from the 1878 geological maps of Dr. G.M. Dawson and from brief surveys of old Indian Reserves also made about that time, as well as from a few old timber leases and sales of earlier years. A more recent blueprint, made in 1907, came from the extensive staking done by the timber cruisers of the Graham Steamship, Coal and Lumber Company of Los Angeles. They had staked claim to most of the merchantable timber in sight on the north and mid-sections of Graham Island, and had included in the claims the waterfront so vital to the transportation needs of the settlers. These claims, although unsurveyed, were recorded and shown on the 1907 blueprint but were later found to be full of inaccuracies.

It was to Charles Harrison, the only local authorized government official, who everyone had to go to complete their preemption application. He was also the salaried agent of the timber company and as such had the only 1907 blueprint in the area. With company wishes in mind, he did his best to persuade applicants for land anywhere near timber claims that the land was not available—the company having made it clear that it was not receptive to settlers adjacent to their property—and he successfully diverted a number of people from their first choice. But when land surveyors commenced working in the region, information became much more reliable.

Fred Nash began a survey on the south side of Delkatla Slough following his completion of the North Beach assignment, and from his maps Trevor and Francis learned that there was unstaked acreage available near their camp. Francis applied for this. Trevor really liked the Massett Inlet country better. Finding that there was a vacant site about a mile north of Eli Tingley on the waterfront, he staked his preemption and filed for that place.

Putting his newly-acquired skills to use, he built a log wall to a three-foot height and set his eight by ten-foot tent on top of this. A pole floor was laid, rough bunk and table constructed, and the collapsible stove installed with the stove-pipe going through an asbestos ring in the tent roof.

"My darling Meta," he began, as he set about explaining his plans, "I have 160 acres extending for about one mile east and west, across the middle of a peninsula. There is waterfront on both ends. I'm going to build a log house near the shore on the west side, where I now have my tent pitched. The view over the Inlet is superb from here and the sunsets, even at this time of year, are magnificent. The same is true of the moon at night when it sends great shimmering reflections across the water. Incredibly beautiful.

"I am amazed at the variety of trees on this place—some enormous cedars, spruce, hemlock, and a few pine as well as alder and even some yews. The alder is particularly valued as firewood, although it must be well-seasoned for this. To build the walls of the log house I'll need cedar trees, not too large, probably about a foot in diameter and as even-shaped as possible. These are cut into appropriate lengths, then laid horizontally one upon the other, with notches at the corners to fit and hold the logs securely. They are pretty awkward for one man to manoeuvre, so neighbours help one another with the actual building.

"I have a good spring which supplies my water requirements. This comes from a natural meadow about four hundred feet from where the house will be. The beach in front here has small boulders along the top, but these soon give way to sand—not unlike the sand beach between Swansea and Mumbles. There are a few scattered boulders on this sand, but it will be simple to clear a passageway to bring my boat in and out safely.

"From my tent door, which faces the water, there is an abundance of game—unacquainted with hunters. At high tide I can shoot all the ducks and geese needed without even leaving the tent! To give you an idea, I got three geese today with just one shot. So with a sack of onions and a case of dried apples, I will have as much roast goose and applesauce as I can eat as well as some for my neighbours."

It was some months before he had a reply to this, which was not unexpected owing to the difficulties of mail service. Nevertheless, he agonized over the length of time. Was it significant?

At last the envelope with the beloved handwriting arrived. Her letter was full of the doings of friends in Swansea, some office news, and a bit about an art class she had joined. She politely commented on his new venture. But that was all. Well, what the devil did he expect anyhow? It would be a miracle if their relationship continued. . .

He threw himself into the business of homesiting with all the vigour of youth and tried not to think about the possible eventuality that his choice of a future on these Queen Charlotte Islands could cost him dearly.

SEVEN

THE 1908 SOLITUDE OF Massett Inlet was not to last. As land seekers flocked to the Charlottes in a steady stream, it was inevitable that they would also filter into the Massett Inlet area. This urge to own a piece of land—any kind of land—was undoubtedly due to the depression of the preceding twelve months, which had thrust so many thousands into insecurity. British Columbia Government pamphlets flooded the country, offering "Free land—just for the taking..." and extolling the rewards which could be had with little or no effort, particularly on Graham Island.

The peninsula which extended north from Eli Tingley's preemption was now fully staked. Arthur Robertson, a former Shetland Islander, built a cabin at the head of the bay near the east side of Trevor's land, and another Scot, Charles Adam, preempted the entire north end of the peninsula which adjoined Trevor's north boundary. Between Trevor and Eli Tingley were Gus Lundquist, R. Gilmark, and Trevor's erstwhile prospecting partner, Charlie Copp. Copp had left with Davies following their prospecting venture, but in Port Simpson he heard rumours of an impending land boom on Graham Island. He returned to the Massett Inlet area to put in stakes near Eli and also at Mayer Lake, which he had reached by hiking east along the Mexican Tom Trail. Then he left for Vancouver to raise capital to expand his speculative enterprise at Mayer Lake. Gilmark never returned after his initial staking, and none of them ever heard of him again.

With men coming in ever-increasing numbers over the Mexican Tom Trail to look for land, Eli Tingley's cabin was constantly full-to-bursting with visitors, so Eli asked Gus Lundquist, the Swedish ex-sailor who was an excellent carpenter, to help him build a smaller cabin for use as a guest house to ease the situation. Trevor went to give a hand lifting the logs for the upper part. He told Gus he wanted to build a fourteen by sixteen-foot cabin but, instead of the usual one-story, thought to make it one-and-a-half so as to have a bedroom upstairs. "Would it present difficulties in construction?" the novice asked Gus.

"Well...not really," Gus replied. "Just be sure the foundation logs sit square on the ground. I'll give you a hand in a few weeks if you like."

In anticipation, Trevor had sent to Vancouver for tools to use in his homesteading enterprise—saws, mattock, claw-hammer, sledge-hammer, wedges, froe for splitting shakes, plus other smaller tools not obtainable locally. There were two small general stores on the Massett Haida Reserve, Henry Edenshaw's and Henry White's. These two men also owned the two schooners which plied between Port Simpson and Masset. The tools would be shipped to Port Simpson, then sent to Massett on one of the schooners with any other mail or freight for the north end. The various items would be left at either of the stores to be picked up by the owners when they came in for supplies and mail.

There was a warm feeling of camaraderie as the settlers cleared the land and put up cabins, everyone freely helping his neighbours without hesitation. The sound of axes ringing sharply in the frosty air became familiar as trees were felled and cabin logs made ready for skidding to a chosen site. Thick clouds of pungent smoke hovered atop huge stacks of evergreen branches piled high for burning. As the first few fragrant boughs ignited, smoke gave way to a shower of sparks, and flames soared skyward with a rush. Trevor soon found that his recently-acquired tools were of value not only to himself, but also to his neighbours—anyone within five or six miles. As an added bonus, when loaning tools and going along to help, he received much in the way of valuable advice to offset his inexperience in their use.

The rudimentary knowledge he acquired in handling his boat in the winds and tides of the capricious Inlet was to be upgraded that winter by those capable teachers, "trial and error." With few boats in the area he was frequently in demand by land survey parties to keep their crews supplied. This meant many trips to the Massett Reserve, twenty-eight miles away. The sixteen-foot Linton rowboat, which always carried two pairs of oars, a detachable mast, boom, sprit-sail, rudder, grub-box, axe, and blankets, could make fairly good time with oars or sail when tides and winds were right. It could carry three or four passengers or six to seven hundred pounds of supplies. With favourable winds it would take four or five hours of sailing and in calm weather, five to six hours of rowing. With head winds it could be ten to twelve hours or perhaps even two or three days when he had to lay-over on the way waiting for weather.

There were several camping places en route belonging to the Massett Haida but commonly available to all travellers. These had the usual rough shelter—pole frame covered with bark or shakes, one door, and a hole in the roof over the fire-pit in the centre of a dirt floor. When delayed by adverse weather the boat could be landed, emptied of gear and supplies, and hauled above the high-tide mark. Wood and water had to be procured, often in heavy rain, so the shelter of the Indian camp was appreciated to the full. Only once did Trevor have to spend a cold, miserable night under a tree. Once was enough. He soon learned to arrange an enforced shore stay to coincide with one of the camps.

He would never forget one particularly memorable trip. Alone in the boat, with a minimum of sail, he was sitting on the high side of the heeling craft, hanging on to the straining boom rope. Without warning a sudden change of wind brought the boom so swiftly across to the opposite side that he went overboard as the boat half-filled with water. He was wearing the thick clothing needed for winter sailing in an open boat, plus cumbersome, leather hip-length seamen's boots and a long, heavy cavalry cloak. With boom, sail, and himself dragging alongside, he travelled three or four miles before he succeeded in pulling his sodden weight into the boat and was able to seize the rudder and steer for shore. By sheer luck he was then at the Massett Reserve. Another half mile would have taken him out to sea. Indians came down to help him empty the boat then drag it up above the high-tide mark. Trevor was too paralyzed by cold to be of much use. They took him to the Edenshaws where kind, motherly Mrs. Edenshaw put him into a warm bed, then took his wet clothing to dry. It was a close call.

In another gale, with two men on board as ballast, he had made the trip to the Reserve in slightly under four hours—a record. They had to bail most of the way as spray and heavy rain kept filling the boat. He was learning a lot about handling the Linton in rough weather, but it was fortunate he had such a seaworthy craft.

Gus Lundquist came to help build the Williams' cabin as promised and brought some interesting news. Bert Tingley, Allan Stewart, and Emerson Calhoun had arrived and were going to help Eli put up an eighteen by thirty-foot log house on the point west of his cabin. (The guest house built by Gus was much smaller and had been put on the east side of Eli—close by a stream.) "Going to be a store and post office as soon as he finds someone to run it," said Gus. Trevor joined him in a chuckle at Eli's optimism. Store and post office out in the bush?

But they had underestimated their neighbour. As soon as the new log house was up, Bert, Stewart, and Calhoun hiked the forty miles to Skidegate to catch the *Amur*, and Eli followed a few days later. In Vancouver he met James Martin who had recently sold his store on the prairies and was looking for a good place to locate on the coast. Eli's eloquence persuaded this extremely shrewd businessman to go north— sight unseen—with a complete stock and the material to build and operate a general store in that wilderness location.

Trevor, *left*, persuaded Gus Lindquist to help him build his log home, which was to be storey-and-a-half instead of the usual one-roomed cabin. He also sent for a selection of tools and in going along to help when they were borrowed, picked up tips in their use.

James Martin's launch *Kathleen*.
Photo–Mabel Nelson

The nicely-built frame store of James Martin in the embryo townsite of Queenstown, Masset Inlet, 1909. Log building on the left is the townsite's hotel, built by Eli Tingley to cope with the steady stream of landseekers. Photo–Dr. Graves

James Martin, the very shrewd storekeeper, who was persuaded by Eli to bring materials and stock for a store, sight unseen, to the wilds of Masset Inlet.
Photo—C. Martin

This photo was taken by Trevor Williams, who had written on the back, "Caught by Eli Tingley, a neighbour of mine, in Masset Inlet, 1909—in a small skiff. No scale, but estimated to be over 200 lbs." The photo was taken in front of Eli's cabin. Eli is the man on the left.

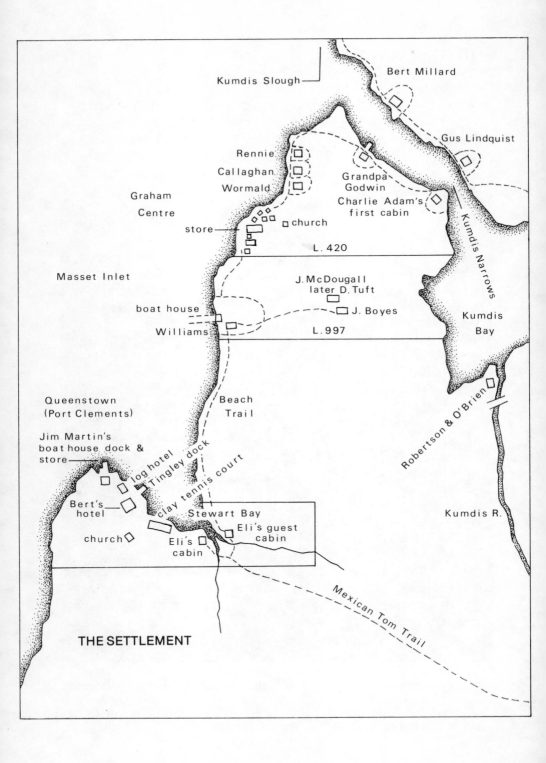

Kumdis Slough

Bert Millard

Gus Lindquist

Rennie
Callaghan
Wormald

Grandpa
Godwin
Charlie Adam's
first cabin

Graham
Centre

store

church

L. 420

Masset Inlet

J. McDougall
later D. Tuft

J. Boyes

Kumdis
Bay

boat house

Williams

L. 997

Kumdis Narrows

Beach
Trail

Queenstown
(Port Clements)

Robertson & O'Brien

Jim Martin's
boat house dock &
store

Kumdis R.

log hotel
Tingley dock

clay tennis court

Bert's
hotel

Stewart Bay

Eli's guest
cabin

church

Eli's
cabin

Mexican Tom Trail

THE SETTLEMENT

"December 12, 1908" Trevor entered in his diary. "Looked across to Stewart Bay and couldn't believe my eyes. Anchored off Tingley's point was a veritable flotilla. Two Haida schooners, Edenshaw's *Josephine* and Henry White's *King George*, together with Tingley's big Columbia River boat, plus a gas boat, the *Kathleen*. The *Kathleen* had a fair-sized raft of lumber in tow.

Going over to greet the new arrivals he found that the newcomers included Jim Martin, owner of the *Kathleen*, plus two brothers, Frank and Louis "Ole" Van Valkenburg, and a white-headed gentleman, Alfred Carse, a lawyer from Victoria. All hands pitched in to unload the boats, putting the supplies into the big log house which Eli had built for just this moment. "I'll be damned," thought Trevor. "He's actually pulled it off. Good for Eli!"

The following day the *King George* brought more lumber and goods for Martin as well as mail for some of the settlers near-by. This included Trevor's preemption record from William Manson, the Government Agent in Prince Rupert. The application had been sent to Port Simpson, and in the interim the tent town of Prince Rupert had apparently usurped the old, established village of Port Simpson to become the new centre for the north coast.

Well, thought Trevor, just one more in the string of changes taking place. He had even heard that Charles Harrison had peddled that scrub land of his lying opposite where Francis and Trevor had camped in Delkatla, and now a town was proposed for the site. It seemed utterly incredible.

Meanwhile Eli, with a store established and post office to be applied for soon, had to have an official name for his townsite. Martin was asked to do the honours and chose the name "Queenstown" after his home town in Ireland. "Good," replied Eli, and promptly christened his Columbia River boat *Queen* to complement the proposal. A big Christmas dinner was planned to give the whole undertaking a festive launching. Ten men crowded into Eli's cabin for the cheerful celebration—Eli Tingley, Jim Martin, Trevor, Charlie Adam, Arthur Robertson, Gus Lundquist, Frank and Ole Van Valkenburg, Alfred Carse, plus a new homesteader from the mouth of the Yakoun River, Frank Meldon (always called "Muldoon"). Everyone brought a contribution of some sort for the feasting and toasting which marked the debut of the new town of Queenstown on Graham Island.

EIGHT

TREVOR'S CELTIC ANCESTORS had bequeathed to him the love of singing which is innate to all the Welsh. "Never hard to find Williams," his neighbour, Charlie Adam, would say. "You can hear his singing a quarter of a mile away," referring to the resonant baritone giving full rein to the songs of his Welsh homeland. The outdoor life and the stimulation of working his own land seemed to give special impetus to this need to sing, and with no near neighbours, he felt he could indulge whenever the spirit moved.

"*20th Jan. 1909*" he entered in his diary. "Art Robertson and Charlie Adam walked by my tent on their way to Martin's store. I was in the woods getting a log ready to add to the wall on the south side, so didn't see them, nor they me. But they said they heard me 'singing my head off.' Ah, well. . . On their way back they helped me wrestle the log to the water and bring it to the new cabin site where we hauled it up. I gave them dinner and, as the tide was still fairly high, took them round to Kumdis Narrows in my boat. Spent the night with them in Charlie's tent on a brush bed on the floor. As only Charlie had blankets, and it was freezing, it was too cold to get much sleep.

"*Jan 21*: Heavy snowfall during the night—about two feet on the ground. Helped Art and Charlie put up the rafters in Charlie's cabin, which is on the hill overlooking the Narrows. Came home to my tent and caught up on sleep.

"*Jan 22*: Art and Charlie had lunch with me. They were using Art's boat which had been frozen in the Kumdis River for the past month. Helped me haul up another log, and Charlie borrowed my mattock."

In addition to the companionship which developed as the young men helped one another with work on their homesteads, there were also the lively bridge games usually held at Tingley's that winter. Martin, Carse, the two Van Valkenburgs, Trevor, and whoever else happened along would deal out the cards, and the hours would seem to melt as the spirited bidding went on. This could mean a rough walk home with a lantern along the dark beach afterwards, but it seemed to be taken in stride. And if there was a particularly vile day, sleet, driving rain, and so on, they would often gather around the stove and put in the day playing cards. Strange it was always bridge they played, thought Trevor.

On one such afternoon, late in February of 1909, they had gathered at Eli's. The weather was appalling. Rain bucketed down, interspersed with icy ribbons of sleet, driven almost sideways by strong gusts of wind. It was impossible to work outside and expect to accomplish anything. Frank Van Valkenburg, filling a pail of water from the creek for the endless mugs of tea that were part of these bridge sessions, thought he saw a boat coming across the Inlet. Disbelieving, he called the others. Straining to see through the haze, they confirmed that it was indeed a boat, with two figures making a valiant attempt to row, but obviously almost exhausted. They seemed to be heading for the point by Martin's store.

Throwing on rain gear, the watchers ran to the beach to secure the boat and lift the semi-frozen visitors ashore. They were astonished to find Reverend W.E. Collison from the church at Massett and Bishop du Vernet from Prince Rupert. The two clerics had left Massett early that morning in their open boat prepared to row the twenty-eight miles to Queenstown and hold a service. Some Divine Power must surely have shepherded them. It seemed a miracle that they had completed the journey on such a day and in such a small craft.

After mugs of steaming tea, great portions of Eli's goose stew, and dry, warm clothing to replace their own saturated garments, feeling gradually returned to their numbed limbs. Then the first church service to be held in Eli's new townsite took place in Jim Martin's recently completed frame store building. Regardless of religious affiliation, all the men turned out, appreciating to the full the discomfort which had been endured to give them the opportunity to take part in the liturgy of divine worship.

"*March 1, 1909:* Gus and Eli came to help me put the last logs up for the walls of my house," was the entry Trevor put in his diary. "It is eleven feet high—the tallest log structure around." Charlie Adam had finished his smaller cabin a few weeks earlier and was already moved in. Martin's store, with shelves and counters installed, was ready for occupancy, and he had moved from the log house Tingley had built for him to use temporarily and was living in the new building. Mr. and Mrs. Bert Millard, who had been among the settlers living on the west side of Massett Sound when Trevor camped in Delkatla, had left that place and applied for land at the north entrance to Kumdis Bay, not far from Charlie Adam. While they waited for their preemption application to be processed, they had agreed to Eli's suggestion to operate a hotel in the log house just vacated by Martin. There were so many people coming through to the area now, this would be a boon.

It was Mrs. Millard who commented on the size and design of Trevor's log house. "Doesn't look like a bachelor's place," she said. "Do you have a wife?" Trevor looked at her. "I'm not married," he answered. But she persisted. "Well...you must have a sweetheart somewhere," she said. "All these other fellows have one-room cabins. Yours is more a family-looking place...upstairs and all. I want Bert to build one like that for us." Trevor was glad she appeared to change the line of conversation. He didn't dare think about why he was building that type of house—this was during the long months when he was waiting for Meta's reaction to his description of the place and decision to take up land.

Among the new arrivals who would figure significantly in local activities were Geordie McQuaker and Alex McTavish. Geordie found land near Frank Meldon at the mouth of the Yakoun River but developed such an affinity for Charlie Adam that he seemed to spend most of his time helping him. Alex McTavish was a six-foot-two, one-eyed charmer from New Zealand. He was a man of mystery who lived with somewhat of a flourish on money wangled from the assortment of backers of his numerous schemes. Like many entrepreneurs of this type, McTavish was excellent company, and his glib tongue soon dispelled any apprehensions one might have. Rumours abounded as to how he had lost his eye, ranging from a fight over an unfulfilled promise to a lady, to a tussle with a disgruntled backer with an unexpectedly empty pocket. McTavish preempted land on the north shore of Kumdis Bay and put up a crude shelter which he rarely used, but it paid lip-service to the preemption requirements. Because of his interesting personality and congenial disposition he was a welcome visitor at anytime.

"*March 6, 1909:* Met surveyors putting a post on my place yesterday morning. They were men sent out by the Graham Steamship, Coal and Lumber Company 'after the fact' so to speak. Cruisers had staked the land in 1907, and the Company had drawn up blueprints and recorded their claims on the strength of these estimates. Now serious inaccuracies in the descriptions were showing up. And it is bad news for some of us.

"On the maps available when we had staked, all of Eli's land, Copp's, Gilmark's, Lundquist's, and my place were free, but part of Charlie Adam's was covered. With the coming of these surveyors the reverse is found to be true. Adam's is completely free. However, Copp, Gilmark, and Lundquist are totally covered, and some twenty of my 160 acres are affected, and the section of Eli's on which he expects to put his townsite is also covered. It is shattering news as the timber company is making it clear that they will vigorously protest further cutting of trees on any of their claims."

Alfred Carse, the Victoria lawyer who was still visiting Eli, held a meeting to get all those involved to sign a petition which he would present to the British Columbia government on his trip south in a few days. No small part of the problem was directly due to the government's effusive promotion of land settlement without providing adequate information as to what was actually available. This was especially true in Eli's case, as it had been an official in McBride's own office who had steered Eli to his site. There surely was an onus now on the government to see that settlers did not lose out, despite the timber claim of an earlier date, since it was errors in description which were proving of consequence to the people affected.

The twenty acres of Trevor's which were affected included, unfortunately, the choice western part on which he had already built his log home and proposed to develop a garden patch and so on. Luckily he had felled a good number of trees before the surveyors arrived, but he wouldn't be able to do much more until the matter was settled.

"*March* 8: Copp came to see me today. He'd arrived in Massett yesterday on the *Capilano*. A Vancouver real estate company has agreed to pay for the land he staked at Mayer Lake last fall, and it will be put on the market similar to Christie's North Beach venture. He has a crew of twelve to fourteen men with him to do the surveying, but needs three or four back-packers to keep the crew supplied. Pay is six cents a pound for the six-mile hike out to the lake. Wanted to hire me on as a packer. Not too much to do here until we get things in order, and I can use the cash."

Everyone in the party shouldered heavy packs for the initial trip. The Mexican Tom Trail was wet and heavy walking after the recent downpours, so camp was made near the south end of the nine-mile-long lake. The following day two rafts were built to freight supplies and men north along the lake to a tent camp which was put up on the shoreline. This was eventually moved several times as the surveyors ran their lines.

"There were three Massett Indians working with the party," Trevor told Eli later. "Andrew Brown, Bob Bennett, and another man whose name I didn't catch. On that first trip out they seemed astonished at the sight of such a large lake in the interior of this Island despite living all their lives here. Quite a bit of 'ohing' and 'ahing.' Said none of them had previously been very far from salt water."

In between trips to Mayer Lake, Trevor was able to get in some time working on his cabin, and on the nineteenth of March was able to move in. "My first home," he wrote Meta. "Now I'm busy clearing and digging ground for a potato patch."

Charles Harrison paid the Massett Inlet settlers a visit about this time, having heard that some preemptions were on his company's timber licence. Arriving in a canoe with two Haidas to do the paddling, he issued a stern warning to Trevor—who promptly ignored it. Trevor had decided he was not going to have any dealings whatsoever over this matter with Harrison. If Carse was unsuccessful, Trevor would write directly to the principals.

Leaving Trevor, Harrison went to Queenstown and had a long talk with Jim Martin. Here his admonitions found fertile ground. The astute Martin knew that Tingley's deep trouble with the timber claim covering his entire townsite boded ill for the future of his store. As he listened to Harrison's news that surveyors were due in to lay out a townsite three miles south of the Massett Indian Reserve, he was very interested.

"Going to call it Graham City," Harrison told Martin, "after Ben Graham, head of the Graham Steamship, Coal and Lumber Company which owns all these timber claims. Actually the Anchor Investment Company is going to develop the town, but they are a subsidiary of the Graham Company. You'd better move down with us," he advised Martin. "Tingley is finished."

A month later, near the end of April, with no word from Carse and the future of Queenstown still cloudy, Martin announced that he was moving to Graham City. For the time being he would leave Frank Van Valkenburg in charge of the Queenstown store, and Frank would use the Martin launch *Kathleen* to keep the store supplied from the larger one Martin was arranging to build in Graham City. Eli's application for a post office at Queenstown had been rejected as there was already another post office by that name in Canada. Martin, who had chosen the name, was displeased at any thought of dropping it, so to humour him Eli let the Queenstown designation stand for the time being, but it was obvious that sooner or later this change would have to occur.

When Copp, Gilmark, and Lundquist realized that the timber claim covering the land they had staked between Trevor and Eli was not going to be easily dealt with, they abandoned their sites. Only Lundquist restaked in the area, choosing land now shown to be free on the north side of Kumdis Narrows, opposite Charlie Adam's cabin. Trevor and Eli still hoped that something could be done to enable them to obtain clear title to their preemptions, but neither wanted to do much more work without some definite indication that this would happen.

Word from Carse was vague and discouraging, so by the end of June, Eli decided to go to Victoria himself and find out what was going on. "I'm going to take the *Queen* and tie her up in Rupert," he told Trevor. "I want to bring an engine back with me from Victoria, and it will be easier to install it over in Rupert than here. Why don't you come along with me? Can't do much around here for awhile. Change of scenery might do us both good."

Leaving his treasured Linton boat in Tingley's shed for protection, Trevor loaded the necessary camping gear into the *Queen*. With a good wind on the Inlet and an ebbing tide, Eli hoisted the big mainsail, plus a small jib. They left for Massett that same afternoon. At the Nadu the tide had begun to turn, so there was nothing for it but to go ashore and make camp for the night. Here they met a gasboat with men on board making soundings. They told Eli they were part of a hydrographic survey party sent to chart the waters of Massett Inlet and Massett Sound.

"Pressure from the timber company," commented Trevor.

"Has to be," replied Eli.

They had light but favourable winds the following day when they got under way for Prince Rupert, but as they approached Rose Spit a furious southeast gale blew up. Eli decided to turn back to Massett and wait out the storm. It was a rough trip. Half-way there they were surprised to meet Edenshaw's two-masted schooner towing a big Haida canoe and obviously prepared to cross Hecate Strait despite the gale. This was the canoe Alfred Davidson and his younger brother, Robert, had spent the past eight months building for the Seattle Exposition. It was a beauty. Fifty-seven feet long, with a beam of six-foot-four inches—this was a work of art by master craftsmen.

Later they heard that as Edenshaw had rounded Rose Spit, the fury of the gale caught his schooner, and the tow line suddenly snapped. In minutes schooner and canoe were out of sight of one another. Edenshaw had all he could do to guide his boat safely into Prince Rupert after a gruelling trip across the Strait. He tried not to think of the certain drowning of the two Haidas in the canoe. And he could hardly believe his eyes when he saw it safely tied up in the Rupert harbour. It had beaten the schooner by several hours and had had a relatively good trip. When the rope broke, the Haida and his wife in the canoe had quickly hoisted a small sail. The big craft glided easily along the top of the combers, whereas the shorter schooner had ploughed into each and every wave, making heavy going all the way. (*Note:* This was the canoe on exhibition at Canada Place during the 1986 World Exposition in Vancouver, British Columbia. It was on loan from the National Museum in Ottawa.)

"*July 2, 1909:* Tingley and I again set sail for the mainland, having had to wait out the weather at Massett for several days," was Trevor's diary entry. "Had fair wind until we got near the south end of Dundas Island, then the wind suddenly dropped. Using the sweeps we rowed the heavy boat from there to Tugwell Island and found a sheltered spot to anchor in. There was eighteen feet of water under the keel, so Tingley put out the anchor, and we settled down for what was left of the night...bone-tired after the exhausting row." It was 2 a.m.

Awakened by brilliant sun a few hours later, they were aghast to find themselves high and dry on a long reef which extended off Tugwell. A large rock jutted from the ridge

July 1909. Eli's *Queen* tied to a dock in Prince Rupert. Sail drying in the sunshine.

Bill Raymond, *left*, reporter for the *Empire* in Prince Rupert, meets Trevor on Centre Street, to give him a tour of the town. They had last seen each other in Montreal when Trevor worked for the Canadian White Co. and Bill was a reporter for a Montreal newspaper.

July 1909. Skeena River at its junction with the Ecstall. The small Alexandria Cannery shown on left with the outer part of Balmoral Cannery centre and right. Balmoral was the largest cannery on the coast at that time. Trevor worked as a tallyman for Mark English. Prices for fish were one whole sockeye—ten cents each, one spring salmon, red only—thirty cents per fish. White springs were discarded.

More of the Balmoral Cannery, July 1909. But it does not take in the cannery part even so. That is a portion of the net racks shown in lower right, the cannery itself is even further to the right.

Waiting at Martin's small dock. Martin's boat-shed extreme left. Kumdis Island is the headland on right in background. On the left of it is the main entrance to Masset Inlet, from Masset Sound. In photo below, the entrance to Kumdis Slough is seen to the right of Kumdis Island. Sailboat is Eli's *Queen*. Dock is Martin's. George Mayer, standing, facing camera, came to the area in 1907 and built his cabin about two miles to the northeast of here, near mouth of Kumdis River.
Both photos taken by Ole Van Valkenburg

View on Masset Inlet

Eli ferrying passengers in his *Queen* on Masset Inlet.
Photo–Ole Van Valkenburg

Bert Tingley's fine hotel, with verandah facing the water, had an attached
store and post office, with living quarters over the post office.
Photo–B.L. Tingley

barely three feet to one side. "Whew! Lucky we didn't come down on that," Eli heaved a sigh of relief. "Must be a terrific rise and fall of tide in the area—over twenty feet at least, I'd say." As soon as the incoming tide floated them off they sailed through Metlakatla Passage to Prince Rupert where they tied up at a small dock.

Among the people strolling the dockside Trevor saw a familiar face—reporter Bill Raymond—last seen in Montreal. He was now working for the *Empire* newspaper in Prince Rupert. "Told you we'd meet again," said Raymond as he pumped Trevor's hand in greeting. "Come on... I'll give you a tour of the town." The place seemed to be booming: new buildings going up all over, plank walks erected on pilings beside the sturdy trestles over the muskeg for roads. There was a general atmosphere of anticipation.

After Eli left for Vancouver on the *Camosun* the next day, Trevor took the *Queen* to the shelter of Hays Cove to beach her out of harm's way. With a fair-sized creek coming down off a bank close by, it was a good place to camp while he had a look around. "Perhaps I should buy a few lots here," he mused. "If things don't work out on the Charlottes this might not be a bad place to settle... far enough out of the main town."

At a real estate office belonging to David M. Hays, brother of Charles Hays, the moving spirit behind the new city, he described what he wanted and was offered Lots 33 and 34 on the hill behind his campsite. "Your lots face out onto Ambrose Avenue," he was told. "Price, $165 each—with one-quarter down and three years to pay the balance." Trevor signed an agreement to purchase and gave Hays a cheque for $50.

During his walks along the waterfront he met a Mr. Barker who was looking for a tallyman to work at Balmoral Cannery on the Skeena River. He offered Trevor the job.

"*July 9, 1909:* Went with Barker on the tug *Chieftain* to Port Essington, which is known locally as 'Spokeshute,' and from there we went to Balmoral Cannery, the largest on the coast.

"*12th July:* Started to work as tallyman under Mark English, the manager. English is said to have built a hotel at Jedway, near the south end of the Charlottes, although I would say he is most obviously a cannery-man at heart. The only fish accepted at Balmoral are sockeye—ten cents each and springs, red only—thirty cents each. White springs are discarded. Plenty of spring salmon, each weighing a hundred pounds or over, are delivered to the cannery. These are split, boned, and salted and sent to Hamburg."

Eli wrote to say that he was returning to Prince Rupert on August 16th. He was bringing a 3½ horse power Palmer engine for the *Queen* and good news about the timber licence trouble. Would Williams meet him and go back to the Islands?

When Trevor checked into the Grand Trunk Pacific Inn Annex where Eli was staying, there were great doings in Prince Rupert. Sir Richard McBride, Premier of British Columbia, had arrived. Free beer and smokes, singing, Indian bands playing and marching, and much hoopla accompanied the inevitable speeches. Enjoying the festivities was Alfred Carse, who now had an office in Prince Rupert. Carse had found the political odds too formidable to be able to help Tingley in his struggle for a clear title to Queenstown—but he was full of good wishes.

While the engine was being installed in Tingley's boat, a larger one was being put into Henry Edenshaw's *Josephine*. Edenshaw agreed to tow Tingley across the Strait as the weather was uncertain, and Eli had some special passengers— his sister Laura and her friends, May and Ruth Woods, had come to spend a week with him at Queenstown. They got as far as Metlakatla the first night, then it was a grueling twelve hours to the Massett Reserve where they spent the second night, but the ladies insisted it was "just wonderful."

When it was time for the women to return, they were adamant about one thing—they wanted to cross Hecate Strait in the *Queen* under sail. Eli's argument that the *Josephine* would be faster and more comfortable fell on deaf ears. Adventure was what they had come for. "I'm simply going to have to take them," Eli told Trevor. "Will you come with me? If the weather is at all decent I'll just overnight in Rupert, then come right back." It was now the second day of September, 1909, and for once Hecate Strait was in a gentle mood. They enjoyed an excellent crossing both ways.

During their brief stop-over in Prince Rupert, Trevor had lunch with Reverend W.E. Collison, recently transferred from the Massett Reserve and preparing to proceed to Stewart. Collison had been instrumental in obtaining a post office for the Reserve during his last years there, with himself as postmaster. It had been a boon to the area residents.

"Did you know that there are two Massetts now?" he asked. "Yes," he went on, "Harrison wanted a post office for his Graham City, and knowing full well he wouldn't get one with the Reserve office a mere three miles away, the sly old fox quietly changed the name of Graham City to Massett. Then when I left he applied for the job and gave his address as Massett. The government never knew the difference. So the post office will be moved from the Reserve to Harrison's place. Actually, I hear Martin will be the postmaster and run it from his store. Going to be some mix-up with two towns of the same name so close together."

While they were shaking their heads over Harrison's incredible audacity, Collison told Trevor that the Reverend William Hogan was now in charge of the church at the Massett Reserve. Trevor had met the six-foot-four, three-hundred-pound Hogan, a man in his late seventies, in May of 1908, when he, Copp, and Davies had been waiting in Port Simpson for Edenshaw to take them to Massett on their prospecting venture. He had been impressed with the giant parson's sincerity and common sense.

Tingley's good news concerning the timber claims was that the preemptors would be granted clear title to their lands but would not be permitted to cut any trees without special permission from the timber company. However, Eli understood that even this hurdle would be alleviated in the near future. Fortunately for Trevor he had done most of the clearing necessary for his immediate plans, so not being able to cut the remaining timber posed no hardship at this stage. But Eli's townsite was covered with a luxuriant stand of trees belonging to the timber claim. This made it difficult—still he was free to develop a series of acreages around the perimeter of the claim, land which he could market as soon as he obtained his Crown Grant. When a settlement was reached with the company he could develop the townsite proper and choose another name. For now it might as well remain Queenstown to keep Martin happy.

Trevor immediately wrote to Meta describing his elation that he could proceed to develop his property with a free mind. "There's a lot to be done, but at least there's some point to it now. I've been ditching through heavy timber this past week; hard work—but the weather has been excellent. Now I want to continue this ditch all round my garden patch, then put another leading from the meadow to the beach. The meadow is very swampy, so this should help considerably.

"Last week I had an unexpected bonus. A load of railroad ties being towed from the Yakoun to Massett broke away, strewing the beach near my place. As no one seemed interested in rounding them up, I was given permission to pick up what I wanted. Hewn on two sides, they make great building material, and I recovered enough to wall up my woodshed. Looks like a blockhouse—but will be warm and comfortable when the cold winds blow off the Inlet this winter. The ties were destined for Prince Rupert to be used in the building of the Grand Trunk Pacific Railroad, but there was some dispute over payment, and the men who cut them left in disgust."

In far-off Swansea Jack Taylor looked at his sister after she had finished reading parts of the letter to him. "It seems as though Trevor has really found his niche at last," he commented.

"Yes," she replied somewhat wistfully, "it all sounds so exciting. . . I wish I could be there. . ."

"Well, if you wait until Trevor thinks it's grand enough to bring you to, you'll be old and grey and hobbling on a cane," he told her. "He seems to have this daft idea that he must offer you the same as you have now."

"I'm afraid Mother is the reason behind that," Meta answered, "and I don't know how to handle it without making a bad situation worse. She's told him outright that she expects anyone marrying a daughter of hers to provide a good standard of living, and Trevor's pride was really stung as she inferred that he would never be able to measure up in this respect. Now he feels he has to prove he can before marrying me. It's so absurd, Jack. I honestly don't know what to do...When he first got that idea of settling on his own land—I thought he would have said something about our future, but he didn't. Just described how beautiful the place was. I felt really crushed...didn't know how to answer him. So I didn't say too much. Now I wonder if I missed an opportunity...it's so hard to know what to do...."

Her brother put his arm around her. "Well, I'll tell you what you should do. Take matters into your own hands. Write and tell him that now he's settled and has a house you'll be out to marry him in the spring. It's the only way, Meta. Although I shudder to think of what Mother and Father will say. But I'll back you up, you know that. You may as well be there with him as eating your heart out like this. And he is obviously dying to have you, even though he can't say so because of the situation. I think you are mad to wait any longer. But you go out to Canada. Don't let him come back here, whatever you do. Too much chance of a fuss with Mother. That could be disastrous."

Jack is right, she thought. It really is the only way. I have to be the one to make the move. The letter was written that same evening.

It arrived in mid-November. Trevor felt as though he walked ten feet off the ground. Meta...here? Incredible. Fantastic! He read the words again to make sure he had not misunderstood. "Trevor, darling," she had written. "Your news was wonderful. And now that you have established the future of your land and built such a fine house, I'll be able to join you in the spring. What a privilege to be able to build our future together in those lovely surroundings. From your letters I know I will love it all just as you do. Write and tell me what I should bring to keep house in a log cabin...

I'll join you in the spring. What fabulous words. He repeated them again and again.

Then panic struck.

Did she really understand what it would be like? Had he written too glowingly? He looked around the bare walls of his cabin. "My God!" he groaned. There wasn't even any decent furniture—just the home-made utility items he found adequate for his bachelor existence. He remembered the large Taylor home in Mumbles—the big, well-kept garden, tennis court, hot-houses, cook, housemaids, gardener, and so on. Meta's only domestic knowledge was probably dusting the drawing room occasionally. Not much of a preparation for life in a primitive situation like this.

The more he thought about it, the worse it got. He must be completely honest in his presentation of the life she would be coming to...the distances, lack of female companionship— except the motherly Mrs. Bert Millard—unless you went twenty-eight miles in an open boat. Drinking water from a hole in the ground, baths in a small wash-tub, only a small store to shop in—and this carried just the basic necessities. A far cry from the relatively lavish displays of Swansea's shopping districts. If by some miracle, in spite of all this, she still wanted to marry him and live out here, he would come to Swansea. It was unthinkable for her to make that long trip alone.

Then came the even more difficult task as he sat down to write Samuel Taylor.

Meta opened Trevor's letter with shaking hands. She was filled with trepidation about his reaction to her boldness. Then as she began to read his list of the hurdles facing her, she sighed with relief. It was going to be fine.

"I realize there will be many new situations to get used to," she wrote in reply, "but I will have such an experienced teacher by my side." As for him coming to Swansea to accompany her on the trip to Canada... "Mother and Father would insist on a huge wedding with all the trappings and fuss. I couldn't escape this, and I'm sure both of us would hate it. Why don't I meet you in Vancouver? It seems much simpler. I can certainly manage on my own for that part of the journey...especially when I know what lies at the end."

In addition to Jack's advice that they must keep Trevor and her parents apart at this stage, it also seemed utterly foolish to Meta that Trevor should spend so much on a return trip to Wales from those far-off Queen Charlotte Islands when money was such a besetting problem for him. And the

"I'll join you in the spring," Meta wrote Trevor in the fall of 1909, and enclosed this photo.

Trevor suffered an agony of apprehension as he waited for her reaction to the wilderness life he found so satisfying.

Mrs. Charles Harrison, dark dress, beside Mrs. William Hogan. Seated are May Hogan, William Hogan and a friend of May's, who was visiting the Hogans at Masset.

Father Hogan was the greatly esteemed Anglican parson who stood six-foot-four and weighed upwards of three hundred pounds. The Hogans came to the Masset Haida village in 1909.

The Ives Hotel in Masset was where Trevor stayed on his trips for mail and supplies. The man beside the children, who has his hands on his hips, is Gus Lindquist. Trevor stands third from the right, no hat. Beside him, second from right, is the portly "Cap" Francis, who came to Delkatla in 1908 and anchored his sailboat beside Trevor's temporary camping site.

Masset—1909. Charles Harrison stands in the gateway, his newly-built house in the background. Mrs. Harrison is kneeling in the garden.
Photo—C. Ives

Volunteers made a good clay tennis court in Queenstown, which was in constant use. It was to the east of Bert Tingley's Hotel. (Today the Port Clements Museum is close by the area.)

Spectators wait for a turn. Shown here left to right are Eli Tingley, Ruth Woods (whom he later married) and Meta Williams, with racquet. Eli's sister Laura is on the big spruce block used as a roller for keeping the court in good shape.

arguments she was having with her parents these days after breaking the news that she planned to go to Canada and marry Trevor had become so exhausting, a big wedding was absolutely the last thing she wanted to face. To be on their own for this ceremony would be heaven. She still remembered the fuss and furor when her sister Freda had married Vipont Lewis, scion of the Lewis Lewis store in Swansea. It was awful. Even though it had been three years earlier, the entire Taylor house had been in an upset for ages it seemed and still hadn't properly settled down. With the frayed nerves of another big wedding, someone would be bound to say something which might offend Trevor's understandable pride. It would be much better for everyone if he didn't come to Swansea at this stage. Her parents would eventually come round, she felt sure—but it would take time.

Somehow Samuel and Molly Taylor always thought Meta would forget about this man she had been yearning over for so many years and who seemed to be bent on searching for lord-only-knows-what at the very ends of the earth. "Out of sight, out of mind," Molly had said hopefully as the time passed and there was no sign of Trevor at the door. "How can she wait so long for such an unlikely candidate when there are so many more attractive suitors here? You know...I really did think that young art teacher, Davies, might be in the running. Especially when she accepted that fine, big water-colour he did for her of Caswell Bay. He was a nice lad and seemed to have a future...I've heard very complimentary opinions of him and his work. Supposed to have had some excellent commissions—very well-paid apparently. Meta is dear girl, Samuel, but how can she be so stubborn? Perhaps when she sees that wilderness hut she'll come to her senses."

Samuel Taylor sat puffing on his pipe but didn't answer his wife. Actually, he secretly admired Trevor for his courage in going after what he wanted and not just accepting the tried and true. It took more pluck than he, himself, possessed, he mused. He liked to keep cautious feet firmly together and know exactly what he was getting into. Didn't think he'd ever done anything venturesome on an impulse. The boy had a lot of personality, too. But Samuel Taylor had an especially soft spot for Meta, the eldest of the four children born to him and his first wife, Maggie Jane. Meta was not quite ten when Maggie died with the birth of their fourth child. A few years later he had married the statuesque Mary "Molly" Mulholland, a cousin of Maggie's. Molly had been a good mother to his children and had subsequently presented him with three more to add to their brood. However, there was a bond between Meta and himself which Samuel didn't understand completely. Perhaps it was because she bore such a marked semblance to the petite Maggie and had so much of the same blithe spirit and quick wit which had so captivated him. She had a lot of Maggie's independent nature also—this was obvious now.

Molly said he spoiled his eldest daughter, and perhaps he did. There certainly was going to be an emptiness in his life when Meta left. Yet he had to admit Trevor had written very candidly about the conditions. Now Samuel would have to reply.

The letter was very stilted. Samuel was not good at this. He was giving his blessing to Meta's going, he wrote, because he knew it would be useless to do otherwise. She had made up her mind despite all odds. "When she sees what the circumstances are really like out there she may not want to stay," he warned, and added that he relied on Trevor to arrange her passage home to Swansea immediately if this should be the case.

For the next few months the patience of the cook in the Taylor household was tested severely as Meta tried her hand in that department. She was badgered for advice as Meta made and remade favourite dishes to try to get them just right. However, recipes used in cooking for a household of fourteen or fifteen required considerable adaption to be used for two. This meant the purchase of more appropriate cookbooks and a great deal of coaxing by Meta to fit in the experiments without completely disrupting the kitchen schedule.

The months were also a frenzy of activity for Trevor as he prepared for Meta's arrival. Rolls of thick building paper were obtained from Martin's store. "Thank goodness your lot came in light grey," commented Mrs. Millard. "Much nicer than that dismal dark blue stuff he usually stocks." With help from Charlie Adam to keep the paper straight while it was tacked on with large, flat-headed nails, the walls of the cabin were made neat and snug. Under Gus Lundquist's guidance a stairway replaced the ladder by which Trevor clambered upstairs each night. Gus also helped install a couple of skylights in the roof of the "blockhouse" woodshed and convert it to a kitchen. Another window in the door entering this room, facing west, plus two small ones at the back, improved the lighting considerably. Adjoining this was the new woodshed to house his stack of neatly piled firewood and, at Mrs. Millard's suggestion, a privy was built at the end of the woodshed, protected from the weather. "You men seem to want to put these things a quarter of mile away," she told him. "It means we have to put on boots, coats, and even raingear just to answer a simple call of nature." In reply to his dubiousness at having the "convenience" so close to the house, Mrs. Millard advised, "Oh, just throw a few cups of lime in every so often, and you'll never know it's there. Your wife will bless you for it, believe me."

On the 18th of February, 1910, Trevor made one of his numerous trips to Massett for supplies and mail and found a letter from Meta waiting for him saying she was leaving Liverpool on the *Lake Manitoba* on the sixteenth of March for St. John, New Brunswick. He cut his Massett visit short. There was still plenty to do on the cabin to make it ready for the new occupant, and he should leave for the mainland by the end of this month. With transportation a dicey thing in winter months he wanted to get away in plenty of time to be in Vancouver and have all wedding plans well in hand when she arrived.

NINE

ELI ALSO WANTED TO GO to Vancouver about this time and suggested to Trevor that they take the *Queen* as far as Prince Rupert then catch a steamer south from there. They left Queenstown on March 1, of 1910, hoping for decent weather. It was not to be. Snow and gales forced a lay-over in Massett for several days during which the *Henriette* arrived on her fortnightly trip. The two men decided to leave Tingley's boat in Massett and take the steamer to the mainland. Little did they realize that trip would take a full six days.

The *Henriette* was ridiculously underpowered. One hundred and sixty feet long, she had been a French barque until 1906 when she had been converted to a twin-screw steamer with the installation of sixteen horse-power engines. In any kind of a head wind she went backwards, despite engines at full-speed ahead.

They left Massett early on March 4th but couldn't get around Rose Spit. They tried again the next day and got as far as Lawn Hill. The following day, March 6th, the sea remained rough. Lowering dark clouds thundered over them, sending in light snow flurries and making the sea ink-black in contrast to the whitecaps. Captain Buckholtz nursed his rolling ship as far as Skidegate and the newly-created Queen Charlotte City. Going ashore in this latter place to stretch his legs, Trevor met Windy Young, editor of the *Q.C.News* and sales manager for the townsite. "A match for Charles Harrison in his sales tactics," Trevor told Eli.

Leaving Queen Charlotte City they were barely out into Skidegate Inlet when a stiff breeze blew up, forcing them to anchor for the night in Alliford Bay. On March 7th they proceeded to Pacofi, Lockeport, Ikeda Bay, and Jedway, where they again met head winds and had to anchor. Finally, lumbering and pitching in the gale-force winds they crossed Hecate Strait and arrived in Prince Rupert early on March 10th. "She probably did a lot better with her sails than with those absurd engines," was Eli's opinion as he joined Trevor on deck to watch the docking.

They caught the *Camosun* to Vancouver, arriving in the middle of March. Trevor hurried to the General Delivery wicket in the post office and was given a letter from Meta. She would be in St. John on March 27th, coming on the *Lake Champlain*, not the *Manitoba* as first thought. And she thoughtfully enclosed a strip of paper cut to the size of her finger for a ring. "Bless you," thought Trevor.

"*March 25, 1910:* Waiting in Vancouver. Got a room at 618 Jervis Street and bought the ring. Also bought a bowler hat, white shirt, and blue suit—many years since I've worn such things. Took out life insurance policy with Imperial Life for $1000 after passing a stiff medical and got a marriage licence from the Court House.

"Met a number of people, including Jim Martin's wife who, with her six children, is going to join Jim in Massett. Very nice family. I visited them several times. Saw quite a bit of Sidney Wilson, the accountant with whom I worked in Montreal, and McLatchy—now a school teacher—who also worked with me in Montreal. Met my old friend, Waters, the Baldwin engine man, last seen in Parana, Argentina and now driving a cab here in Vancouver. Also met Appleyard, a fellow trooper last seen in South Africa. Mr. and Mrs. Alan Jessup, a surveyor I'd known at Massett Inlet, invited me to their home in North Vancouver. Rented a bike and got my exercise following

Sidney Wilson on his horse round Stanley Park.

"March 28, 1910: Telegram from Meta to say she had left St. John on CPR train on the 27th and expected to arrive in Vancouver first of April. Hunted for a minister of the Congregational Church, to which all the Taylors belonged. There are at least three such churches in Vancouver, but all ministers seemed absent. Finally located Rev. Merton Smith who agreed to perform the ceremony, but as it might be difficult to get out to his house, he suggested using the Knox Congregational Church downtown. Got McLatchy and Waters to promise to be witnesses. Checked with the CPR train and found train would be arriving on April 2nd. At least we miss April Fool's Day for our wedding! Phoned minister about change of day. It is three and a half years since I last saw Meta, so there is some nervous wondering.

"April 2: Meta arrived at the CPR station in Vancouver 12:20 p.m. with much baggage, smiling and serene after her jaunt, alone, across the Atlantic and this continent. A really marvellous little person. Collecting her baggage, we drove to the church where the Rev. Merton Smith married us—making me the most fortunate man in the world."

Meta would long remember that arrival. She had expected to go to a hotel where she would change into the chic grey suit and smart hat she had spent days selecting from Ben Evans' store in Swansea. Instead, Trevor, after hugging and kissing her soundly, had rushed her to a cab and directed the driver to "Go. Please! As fast as you can! To the Knox Congregational Church." Then to Meta, "Well, you see, I've locked the parson in the church, and I've already been a bit long in getting back." When Trevor changed the day, the minister had been noticeably hesitant. He had a funeral scheduled for about that time and seemed nervous about any delay. Trevor had left McLatchy and Waters with him in the vestry—then as an added precaution, turned the key in the lock. He didn't want any vital slip-ups at this stage. Fortunately, McLatchy and Waters were able to keep the Rev. Merton Smith engaged in spirited conversation, and Trevor's act of panic was never discovered.

So with a smudge of train soot on one cheek and wearing

her dusty travelling costume, Meta was hurried to this ceremony for which she and Trevor had been waiting all their adult lives. Trevor was holding her so tightly it is doubtful he knew what she was dressed in anyhow.

After a week of honeymooning in Vancouver the newly weds boarded the *Princess Alice* for Prince Rupert where they spent a few days in the Grand Trunk Pacific Inn waiting for the *Henriette*'s regularly scheduled trip to Massett.

Trevor had considerable business to see to in connection with the Massett Inlet Settlers Association, so taking time out from his honeymooning he visited the Government Agent and Land Commissioner. From there he went to see William Manson, MLA, to give them first-hand details regarding alienation of land by coal and petroleum speculators. Following the interview, Manson immediately sent a telegram to Victoria urging prompt action to alleviate the situation.

The Settlers Association had been formed on January 14, 1910. Twenty-seven members were enrolled, and each paid $1.00 membership. Trevor was elected secretary-treasurer. Initially the Association's goal was the curbing of indiscriminate granting of coal licences, which not only gave the holder the right to underground resources, but also permitted surface control of hundreds of acres. These licences, which interested speculators only, were a sore point with land seekers now arriving in a steady stream. With the isolated exception of the drill being operated by the Merrills for the BC Amalgamated Coal Company, no legitimate work or prospecting was being done on any of the licences, yet they alienated land needed by settlers. In addition to this problem the Association intended to press for roads and bridges urgently needed in the area.

The passenger accommodation on the *Henriette* was full for the trip to Massett. Captain Buckholtz took the ship out of the harbour late on the evening of April 13th and headed for Edye Passage. Encountering winds off Refuge Bay, Porcher Island, he was forced to anchor there for all of the 13th and 14th and while at anchor picked up a party of ten surveyors and took them aboard. They had left Prince Rupert for Masset on the 10th, on the launch *Tasmania*, but were unable to cross Hecate Strait due to the weather. With additional passengers the *Henriette* was really jammed, but everyone seemed in good spirits—card games were set up, stories of experiences exchanged, and so on. The diminutive Meta took it all in her stride. Trevor nearly burst with pride as he introduced "My wife..." and thought that she charmed everyone with her special grace. Early on the 16th the ship finally left for Massett and arrived there late in the evening—three days this time for the trip.

The two Massetts were being differentiated by calling the Indian Reserve "Old Massett" and Harrison's townsite "New Massett." Later, due to postal confusion when mail destined for Merritt, BC was too frequently sent to Massett, the Massett Post Office was ordered to drop one "t," thus the spelling "Masset" came into use and was ultimately applied to all the features named Massett, such as Masset Inlet, Masset Bar, and so on. "Massett" with the "tt" ending is still used by many old timers, however.

New Masset appeared to be booming. It was being developed by the Anchor Investment Company, a Winnipeg firm headed by Jack and Bill Cook, on land bought from Harrison by the Graham Steamship, Coal and Lumber Company. A new frame house had been built for Harrison to his specifications as part of the deal, and the Harrisons had moved into this comfortable place on the edge of Delkatla Slough's north shore. The Harrison house was soon a centre of hospitality. The understanding help and advice of Mrs. Harrison was greatly valued and long-remembered by many of the early-day brides as she sympathetically eased their transition into the new and strange pioneering life. (For more of Mrs. Harrison's own early days see volume one, page 89–92 of the *Queen Charlotte Islands: 1774 to 1966* by Kathleen E. Dalzell).

The prairie influence of the New Masset developers was most evident in the box-like, flat-roofed structures which were erected along Main Street. One of the buildings, a rattle-trap of a hotel, was sold sight unseen to Arthur Ives and his wife, who arrived with their five children in 1909. Mr. Ives had put his entire life savings into the venture, so despite the inadequacies of the place, had no option but to stay and make the best of things. His well-stocked bar soon became an enormous drawing card.

By the fall of 1909 there was also a small school, a doctor, and of course, Jim Martin's store. Several steamers came into the area now, including the *Henriette*, which had been chartered by the Grand Trunk Pacific for the mail contract. Wharves had been built at both Massets for the steamers to tie to, but the one at New Masset was not far enough out, and occasionally steamers would go aground as a result. Rev. W.E. Collison had run the post office in Old Masset, but upon his transfer to Stewart in the fall of 1909, it would be moved to New Masset, and Harrison could not conceal his impatience for Collison to be off. William Hogan and his wife came from Port Simpson to take over from Collison. Hogan and Charles Harrison took each other's measure, and Hogan was not impressed.

On April 16, 1910, the newly-weds were on deck when the *Henriette* finally tied up to the dock in New Masset. It seemed as though almost the entire populace was waiting near the end of the flimsy structure. Lanterns and "bugs" (a candle set in a can held horizontally to protect it from the wind) were scattered throughout the crowd, and the enthusiastic welcome given the new arrivals was overwhelming. Jim Martin was there to greet his wife and family, and many hands assisted in gathering their baggage for its temporary transfer to the store. The warmth of the reception given also to Meta and Trevor seemed wondrous to Meta. "What incredibly kind people," she wrote her family. "It was as though they could not do enough for us. I felt at home with them immediately."

The numerous boxes and trunks accompanying the Williams' were hauled through the darkness to the Ives Hotel by cheerful, smiling young men—everyone eager to share in the helping. There was a tap on Trevor's arm. It was Mrs. Harrison. "Do bring your wife to tea with me tomorrow," she said. "I'm dying for news from Britain."

Mrs. Harrison and Meta liked each other from the moment of their first meeting, and the hours fairly flew as information was exchanged. Later, as other ladies came to meet the new bride, Meta gradually learned more about this life in the wilds.

Although Trevor's letters had prepared her somewhat for the place, she had not really been able to imagine the reality of Masset. The rough, unpainted wooden buildings, the dirt path for a street, with stumps and jagged roots strewn along the edge, and a thick forest of great trees so close around the small settlement. It was such a contrast to her native land with its tidy brick houses, cobbled streets, neatly kept farms of the country, and the trim lawns and gardens of the towns—with trees only in designated areas. This Masset was new and raw in every sense of the word.

But there was an aura of adventure—almost a glamour. A feeling of being on the brink of history, perhaps even being a maker of that history. The friendliness of people so eager to help one another was enormously stimulating.

The entire experience seemed like a dream. The huge waves of the Atlantic had been frightening, such a vast expanse of nothing but water for days—then the train trip across miles and miles of Canada. The magnificent Rockies! There were mountains in Wales—but nothing on that scale. Then the voyage up the British Columbia coast to Prince Rupert with its planked roads and wooden sidewalks. Meta felt as though she was travelling to the end of the earth. And there was the crossing of Hecate Strait on the *Henriette*. Her skipper was Captain Buckholtz—stockily built, swarthy complexion, and a large handle-bar mustache. He had the swashbuckling manner of a character straight out of one of Jack London's adventure books.

Like many old salts, Buckholtz spent most of his port time in the waterfront bars and wondrous were the descriptions of his narrow escapes from disasters during his years at sea. He didn't always gauge the amount of rum he could handle too well and sometimes boarded his vessel at departure time the worse for wear. So much so that on one occasion on a trip supposedly to Massett, his surprised passengers woke to find themselves tied to the dock at Ketchikan, Alaska. Their skipper had sailed north instead of west.

During the wait for weather at Porcher Island, Meta listened to stories about Captain Buckholtz as well as accounts of violent gales in Hecate Strait, and she grew fearful. But the crossing had been good. Now here she was...almost at the end of her journey. Tomorrow she would see Trevor's beloved homestead. Tomorrow would usher in the true beginning of their lives together after the long year of waiting.

TEN

MASSET SOUND AND MASSET INLET had never looked more beautiful as Martin's launch took the newly-wed Williams from New Masset to Trevor's preemption. It was an auspicious beginning. Mirror-calm water all the way, and the sun shone warmly. It was noon, April 18th, 1910. Frank Van Valkenburg at the wheel hummed and whistled at the pure bliss of a trip to Queenstown on such a day. Meta held Trevor's hand tightly, her brown eyes absorbing all aspects of the lovely waterway—an ecstasy of anticipation growing with each passing mile.

Trevor sat strangely silent. His usual ebullience had given way to an agony of apprehension and dread. What if she didn't like it? They passed Ship Island as they entered the north end of Masset Inlet. The mountains of Juskatla mirrored in the placid waters of the Inlet made a perfect backdrop. Small islands along the shoreline to the west and south of them looked enchanting in the sunlight, and the low wooded expanse of the eastern side seemed lush and pristine. The launch skirted the west side of Kumdis Island, then swung out to clear the straggle of rocks off the south point. "There. That's it...," began Trevor hesitantly. The cabin looked so

April 1910. It was amazing how quickly the rough log house became a comfortable home under Meta's deft hand. She sits outside to admire the sunset and finds pioneering with Trevor to be a thrilling adventure. All traces of the homestead are gone now, and the Abfam Mill takes up a good portion of Trevor's old preemption today with a large loading area on the point between old Graham Centre and the Williams cabin site. And Graham Centre is now part of the Village of Port Clements, which includes all that peninsula in its village boundaries today.

1910. Masset. How the main street looked when Meta first saw it. That's Martin's store on the left with the white sign on its side.
Photo–B.L. Tingley

But a few years later it had lost its rough edges. Martin's store now had a hip roof and was much enlarged. The Ives Hotel is on the extreme right. Man in centre of photo is Chief Henry Weah, of the Masset Haida.
Photo–Mrs. W. Matthews

Boat day. Everyone crowded the rickety dock to meet the fortnightly boat which carried mail, passengers and freight. This is the Grand Trunk Pacific's *Prince Albert* both anchored and tied to the Masset wharf.
Photo–Mabel Nelson

small and the clearing he had made so insignificant among the thick timber of the shoreline. Anxiously he turned to see her reaction.

She was smiling broadly. Oh dear heart!

The launch anchored off the cabin, and as the dinghy made innumerable trips ashore to unload boxes and trunks, the city-bred bride took a closer look at her isolated home in this virgin setting and loved it. This was going to be adventure beyond her wildest dreams.

It seemed incredible to Trevor how quickly the log cabin became a comfortable home under Meta's resourceful guidance. From the capacious trunks came curtains for the windows, books for improvised shelves, tablecloths, china, and silverware—made ready for special dinners. Plus small rugs, cushions, a few vases, and other knick-knacks placed here and there as well as several framed pictures, among them the large watercolour of Caswell Bay done by young Davies for Meta. "It's a beauty!" exclaimed Trevor as he brought it out to be hung. "Who is this fellow Davies?"

"Just a man studying to be an artist," she replied. "I took painting lessons from him for awhile... in a class," she added.

"Another admirer?" teased Trevor with a grin. "Teachers don't usually give their students presents..." Then more seriously, "How many times have we picnicked and bathed on that beach... it's a darn' nice painting, Meta, and thanks to Davies, whoever he is."

The biggest bane for Meta was Trevor's stove—a heater with a drum oven. The oven was heated by the stovepipe running through it, a temperamental thing to use at best. Not too bad for bannock perhaps, but for Meta's inexperienced culinary attempts it became a horror. So the first item on the list for the next trip to Massett was a stove with proper oven and, with the help of the beginner's cookbooks the old cook at home had recommended, she was soon producing successful pies and cakes. Bread, however, was something else. Trevor showed her his method, and lead-like loaves were the result, so it took Mrs. Millard to explain how to accomplish an edible product.

The Millards had moved from Queenstown to their

recently-finished log house near the Kumdis Bay Point and
utilized their two upstairs bedrooms to take in paying
overnight guests. There was no one at all in Queenstown.
However, the key for Martin's store was left with Trevor in
case anyone needed emergency supplies. Eli had gone to the
west coast of Graham Island to prospect with his brother Bert
and a friend, John Coates. He maintained a token residence at
Queenstown to comply with preemption regulations, but his
battle to purchase the timber rights on his place was
deadlocked. In the area, generally, there was a fair amount of
activity—parties of surveyors, both government and private,
were frequently seen, and land-seekers were still coming in.
The Williams seemed to have someone bedded down on their
living-room floor more nights than not, so there was plenty of
company, but except for Mrs. Millard, it was all male.

Trevor planted a garden, and in this he was just as
inexperienced as Meta at cooking. Fortunately, the proverbial
beginner's luck held true, and the vegetables grew well. The
Harrisons had told them about the use of lime, seaweed, and
ashes for a new garden. They explained how to start a compost
pit and advised which were the best vegetables to grow in this
climate, valuable information gleaned from their own many
years of trial and error gardening in Delkatla to produce the
fresh vegetables not otherwise available in isolated areas.

Homesteading activities and the copious correspondence
on behalf of the Settlers Association, plus trips to Massett for
mail, supplies, and social visits for Meta with Mrs. Harrison
and the other ladies, kept Trevor busy. Now in addition he
agreed to take on the task of servicing a tidal gauge on
Richards Island, at the entrance to Jauskatla Inlet. This was a
tedious job as it meant a seven-mile row or sail each way every
five days—no matter what the weather. But there was no one
else to do it, and the information would provide vital local
data.

The CGS *Lillooet*, under Captain Musgrave, had been
detailed to chart the waters of Masset Inlet and arrived on
May 10th to begin the preliminaries. Musgrave, who came to
explain about the gauge to Trevor, was full of resentment at
being sent to Masset Inlet when he felt there was so much

more to be done in travelled waters. However, political pressure on behalf of the Graham Steamship, Coal and Lumber Company, who were proposing a sawmill for either the mouth of the Awun River or the Yakoun, had given the Inlet priority.

The surveyors would set up the gauge, Musgrave said, then the *Lillooet* could depart to finish a survey elsewhere, returning late in September when Trevor would be relieved of his chore. His job was to wind the clock which recorded the times and heights of tidal highs and lows, to remove recorded papers, and to insert fresh rolls. Pay was $30 a month.

So for the next four months, the trip must be undertaken every five days. Meta often went with him. Sometimes they took their blankets and tent, and after fixing the gauge, went further to the west, exploring, fishing, and picking berries. Sleeping on brush beds and cooking over an open fire was truly a novel experience for the former Miss Taylor and brought many "ohs" and "ahs" from her family when her letters arrived to tell them about it.

On one memorable trip early in September, Trevor decided to show Meta Juskatla Inlet. The tide was boiling out through the main channel of Juskatla Entrance, meaning they would have to tow the boat through—Meta along the top of the bank with the rope and Trevor at the water's edge, fending it off rocks. They were nearly through the worst part when one of the strong eddies swung the boat suddenly and he lost his grip. Meta, clambering over a log at that same moment, let the rope slip, and in an instant off went their boat out into the tide-rips and quickly out of sight. There they were—stranded on an island, with no food, water, or coats. Everything was in the boat. The Inlet was empty—no people closer than the Yakoun River, far out of sight.

"There's an Indian cabin at Canoe Pass on the other side of this island," said Trevor. "Let's make for that . . . it will at least be shelter if we have to spend the night out." But as they struggled through the dense salal, thick to the water's edge, he realized no one knew where they were. In the warmth of the early afternoon sun they had shed all but their light clothing—not enough to keep warm in cool night air. The faster they got off that island the better. In a few hours it would be dark.

At Canoe Pass he could see that the water was much too deep and swift to wade at that stage of the tide. "I'll try to rustle up something for a raft of some sort," he told Meta and set off to search for likely material along the high tide mark. Only a few small limbs and bits of bark met his eye for quite a stretch, and he grew increasingly anxious. Time was precious. He didn't want to spend the night out, not with Meta only in a flimsy blouse and light skirt, yet it would be equally risky to be too late getting to the other side and then walking a rocky beach in the dark. Damn! Surely there had to be something they could get across on. A gap in the brush drew his attention as he walked. What was that he could see? Pushing the dense foliage aside Trevor could scarcely believe his good fortune. An old dugout canoe had been hauled up, possibly in the spring, and now was almost covered by the long grass and bushes growing over it. He heaved it over and looked more closely. Pretty rotten, he thought, but with care it might do the trick. Calling to Meta he asked, "It will be nip and tuck. Are you game?" She was.

Dragging it to the water, they cautiously shoved off, and Trevor, using a piece of driftwood, paddled furiously for the far shore. The canoe was almost swamped when they landed, but at least they were safely across and only wet to the thighs. Pulling the old life-saver up into the woods, they gave it an affectionate pat before beginning the long trek to the Yakoun.

It was three hours of exhaustion. Trevor in his heavy, leather seamen's hip boots; "I think they weighed at least ten pounds each," he recalled later, ". . . and were never worn again." Meta, with her skirts sodden around her legs, struggled to keep up the pace. The tide was ebbing, and the beach rocks were slippery. It was almost dark when they reached the Yakoun and another stroke of luck. Edenshaw was anchored in the channel waiting for the tide to turn so he could take supplies to a crew clearing the river of log-jams. He saw their frantic waving and took them aboard and up the river as far as the Indian houses where Trevor was able to borrow a boat and row home. They were both completely done-in after the experience, and Trevor was sorely anguished over the loss of his boat.

The Indian boat had to be returned the next day, but before he took it back Trevor tried to get some of his neighbours to go with him to look for his lost boat. He met with unexpected reluctance. "Oh, Williams...it's a wild goose chase." "You'll never find it now." "It'll have been swept out into Dixon Entrance." "Hopeless!" "Total waste of time..." Everyone balked. Except for Charlie Adam. He came hurrying over. "I'll go with you, Trevor. At least we can look around the Inlet," he said. "It's too bad to lose that good Linton." Taking grub and blankets, not knowing how long the search would last, the two men sailed in Charlie's skiff, towing the Indian boat back to its owner, then set off for a close inspection of the beaches. Barely half a mile from where he lost it, Trevor's boat was high and dry in the mouth of a small creek, completely unharmed and all possessions intact, thanks to unbelievable good luck and an understanding friend.

It was about the end of September when the *Lillooet* returned, and Trevor was relieved of the chore of the gauge. For the next few weeks the *Lillooet's* tenders could be seen moving to various areas in the Inlet, taking soundings and setting up marks on beaches to sight to. The *Lillooet* moved from Ship Island to Ain River, then a little to the west of the Yakoun. It was gratifying to see the big ship moving around and to know that other similar craft would be able to navigate the waters when the work was complete.

Nick Shug, the road foreman from the south end of the Island, visited the Williams near the end of August in 1910 and spent the night with them. "I'm trying to round up as many people as I can to go to Masset tomorrow," he told them. "William Manson, the MLA, Taylor, the Minister of Public Works, and Jennings, the road superintendent for the Islands, are all coming in on the *Bruno* tomorrow. They've agreed to meet with some of the settlers. I think we should really put the pressure on and try to get some action. Alex McTavish will use that new gasboat of his to take us down. Can you make it, Williams?"

"Wouldn't miss it," Trevor assured him.

It was a lively meeting as the forty-three settlers who attend-ed pounded away at the government officials. More roads, more trails, and most especially, immediate action about the coal licences. Let the stakers have underground rights, they said, but for heavens sake free the rest of the 640 acres which each coal licence alienated, and apply some sort of conditions to cut down the abuse evident in indiscriminate staking.

At an earlier meeting of the Association the members had become so irate over the contentious licences they had instructed Trevor to hire a lawyer. He wrote McDonell, KC, but there had been no reply. "Probably wonders where his KC's fee is coming from," said one man. "Or feels we have a hopeless case," replied another. With government officials right here on the spot, it was their best chance to get something done. The Association had been successful in getting the preemption survey fees reduced from fifty cents to twenty-five cents an acre and had been advised that some badly-needed trail work had been ordered. This modicum of progress was encouragement to continue their efforts.

Near the end of September Meta and Trevor visited New Masset intending to stay over only one day, but in the series of gales which swept over the northwest coast, one day became a nine-day visit. Mrs. Harrison would not hear of them being in the hotel for all that time. "Please, come and stay with me," she urged Meta on the third day. "I'd love the company."

It was soon apparent that there was a serious problem in the Harrison home. Charles Harrison was spending more and more time in the hotel bar these days and by night-time was so inebriated he could barely stand. When Trevor went looking for him it meant half-carrying, half-dragging the ex-parson home—with Harrison cautioning Trevor in between bursts of ribald singing, "Shhh! Don't tell my wife..." Lurching in the door Trevor somehow wrestled the errant husband upstairs to bed. It was some job. Through all the commotion Mrs. Harrison sat quietly sewing, pretending not to notice. But when Trevor came down, she said, "Thank you. That was very kind," then carried on with a conversation as though nothing untoward had occurred. How the Harrisons managed when they were on their own, Trevor could only guess. Mrs. Harrison did not discuss the matter with anyone, although her husband's excessive drinking must have been creating tremendous worry.

During this visit Meta saw Dr. Fraser who confirmed that she could expect a baby around the end of January. Meta was totally thrilled. Trevor went into a panic.

"We'd better move to the mainland immediately so you can be near more doctors..."

"No," Meta reassured him. "I like Dr. Fraser. He seems a very competent man. And we have so many good friends here in Masset, it will be much nicer for me. Besides...I don't think I could face Hecate Strait with all these storms. If it would ease things for you a bit, we can come down a few months early. Perhaps stay here for the winter?"

Two of the Kumdis Bay neighbours, Sorenson and Hanson, volunteered to live in the Williams' house—it was much more comfortable than the flimsy shacks they occupied. But finding a house to rent in Masset was difficult. However, in mid-November they finally moved into one on Main Street, opposite the Ives Hotel. It was in deplorable condition, and Trevor had his work cut out mending the leaking roof, putting up a woodshed and new privy, plus cutting enough wood to keep the drafty place warm. The weather was bitterly cold.

Although Meta missed her comfortable log home, she found it a pleasant diversion living in Masset—the community life and so many ladies to talk to. Quite a change from the predominately male visitors of Masset Inlet, kind and thoughtful as they always were. Even Mrs. Millard had left—she was spending the winter with her in-laws in Delkatla.

Delkatla was currently being developed into a townsite by Charles Wilson, a Prince Rupert real estate agent. The land was the former preemption of "Cap" Francis, who had camped beside Trevor there in 1908. Trevor bought two lots in the new townsite as a speculation and in memory of it having been his first camping site after Copp and Davies left. The only access to Delkatla was by boat, but Wilson was supremely confident that a bridge would be soon built to connect his townsite with New Masset. There were already a few cabins in Delkatla, but New Masset had such a head start it was unlikely Delkatla would ever be more than just a residential community.

On December 10, 1910, Trevor obtained his Certificate of Improvement for the Masset Inlet preemption. This was signed by Bert Tingley and Charlie Adam before old Harrison. Now he could apply for his Crown Grant—at long last.

But the real red-letter day came on January 27, 1911, when at 11 p.m. Meta was delivered of their son, with the capable assistance of Dr. Fraser, Mrs. Ives, and Mrs. Bert Millard. Named Jack Morgan Williams, he soon gave evidence of robust lungs, especially so during the nights. Mrs. Millard, who had come to help for a month, soon took over the night shift from the exhausted parents, and there was immediate silence. When she left, Trevor asked how on earth she had achieved such a miracle. "Oh, I just give him a teaspoon of rum in some milk. That soon quiets him down," she told the astonished father.

With the usual worries common to new parents, Meta and Trevor decided to stay in the rented house for a few more months. It was reassuring to have a doctor nearby and other mothers for Meta to visit and talk to. Trevor managed to pick up several jobs to augment their income, and it was not until October of 1911 that they finally returned to the preemption.

Land surveyors were still very much in evidence. Harold Price came to survey Trevor's land for his Crown Grant, and C. de B. "Cedar" Green had done Charlie Adam's. It was said that most of Graham Island had now been surveyed, with survey camps even out around Naden Harbour and the west coast.

The Settlers Association disbanded on April 14, 1911, after a stormy meeting. Trevor had resigned in December of 1910—the position of secretary-treasurer took such an inordinate amount of his time. An election of officers had followed immediately with George Mayer being chosen as president, one of the townsite Cook brothers, vice-president, and O.P Merrill, the coal-drilling and licence representative, as the secretary-treasurer. Trevor agreed to be auditor.

But since neither Cook nor Merrill were regarded as

representative of the majority of settlers, there was tremendous dissension over the election. It had been held during very bad weather, resulting in a poor turn-out of voters. To have a coal licence representative as their secretary-treasurer was too much for most of the settlers who were especially hostile towards the coal licence interests. The fuss became so serious it was impossible to make progress, and dissolving the Association was the only alternative. However, the government announced late in 1911 that no more coal licences would be issued for any land east of Masset Inlet, so perhaps the endless correspondence conducted by Trevor on behalf of the Association had been effective after all. It could not reasonably be expected of Merrill that he would pursue the same tack in view of his interests.

Trevor and Meta were fond of the Merrills, usually calling to visit them at the drill camp south of the Nadu whenever they went to New Masset or home again by way of Kumdis Slough. Actually, the drill camp hadn't operated since February of 1910, but the Merrills were staying on to caretake the premises.

The Williams' were still living in their rented Masset house when Trevor received a letter offering him $1,000 for the two lots he had bought on Ambrose Avenue in Prince Rupert. Since he had only paid a fraction of this, the offer came as a real bonanza. To celebrate he persuaded Meta to accept a long-standing invitation to visit an old Swansea friend now living in Victoria.

She returned from the month-long trip very refreshed. It had been good to see someone from home and talk over old times, but it was also nice to be back on the Islands. And it was wonderful to know Trevor's application for a Crown Grant had been accepted—the title granted free and clear, except for the minor proviso that he was to permit a representative from the timber company access from time to time to cut down trees on the twenty acres included in the company's licence on his land. With the Crown Grant came the official lot number—997.

It was probably about this time that he acquired the nick-name of "Timber Limits Williams," no doubt originating from his long-standing battle for the rights to his land. His initials, T.L. Williams, leading naturally to the sobriquet. Actually, Trevor got quite a kick out of it—particularly now that he had been successful in his struggle.

Eli Tingley had become disheartened with no word as to the outcome of his difficulties with the timber company, but hearing of Trevor's success, he decided to at least go after his Crown Grant and ensure his land. He had heard about the claim-jumping at Kumdis Bay. Arthur Robertson, away looking at likely prospecting sites, had not fulfilled residency requirements needed to obtain title to his preemption at the mouth of the Kumdis River. Taking advantage of this, Edward O'Brian filed on the land, proving that Arthur had defaulted. Arthur's application was cancelled. Then O'Brian nearly had the same thing done to him. Bob Clarke, who had come in with Sid Wormald on a land-scouting trip, liked the O'Brian site as well as any. Hearing that O'Brian spent all his time in Masset, Clarke applied for the O'Brian site using the same reasoning. Fortunately for O'Brian, he was in the Ives Hotel bar when he overheard a discussion by two newcomers. They were talking about the possibilities of claim-jumping and mentioned the ease with which "...that fellow Clarke is going to take over that nice little piece of land at the Kumdis because the owner is spending all his time in Masset." Entering into conversation with the men, O'Brian soon learned the location of "that nice little piece of land." He left Masset early the next morning for the suddenly popular Kumdis site to build a fair-sized cabin and, moving his wife up from Masset within the month, established unmistakable residence, thwarting any claim by Clarke.

With Eli's protracted absences from Queenstown, the same thing could conceivably happen to him if he was not careful. A Crown Grant was a necessity.

ELEVEN

QUEENSTOWN, WHICH APPEARED to be abandoned for
months on end, suddenly began to hum with activity in the
fall of 1911 when an English syndicate announced they were
going to fund the development of a coal licence at Wilson
Creek in the Yakoun Valley. To do this they proposed to build
a thirty-mile road from Queenstown into the site. Burke and
Grey, directors for the syndicate, had visited the region and
gave the go-ahead. The manager, Frank C. Wright, brought
his wife to Queenstown and rented Eli's large log house beside
Martin's store. A Mr. and Mrs. Danbrier moved in with them.
The store, closed for some time now, was also rented by the
company and a small commissary installed with Mr. Kerr as
storekeeper and timekeeper. Green, the superintendent, set
up camp near Eli's first log house and utilized the cabin as a
bunkhouse. A gang of men were soon at work building the
sturdy sleds needed to transport machinery and supplies along
the rough road into the coal location.

In addition to the constant stream of launches coming and
going on the Inlet these days, the Northern Steamships's big
freighter, *British Empire*, poked her nose into the Inlet on
October 24th and anchored for four days off Queenstown

while she unloaded a large amount of machinery and supplies for the coal company. This was the first ocean-going steamship to come into the Inlet since the *Lillooet*, and it created considerable excitement. Anyone who had a boat was welcomed aboard for a visit. Leaving young Jackie with Trevor, Meta accepted an invitation from Mrs. Wright and Mrs. Danbrier to go out to the ship with them.

The Wrights and Danbriers became very friendly with Meta and Trevor, visiting back and forth frequently. And with Mrs. Millard and Mrs. O'Brian close by in the Kumdis, Meta did not lack for feminine companionship now. Each month seemed to bring new arrivals, many with wives and families. There were settlers along both banks of the Yakoun, as well as on the big island at the mouth of that river, with more along the Kumdis Slough, Kumdis Bay, Mayer Lake, and in the Nadu and Watun River areas.

Perhaps the most successful of these homesteaders was Edward Evans at the Nadu. He seemed to know exactly how to coax a living from his fertile land, and in no time, it seemed, there were fruit trees, rhododendrons, roses, and other plants ringing the clearing he and his sons developed for this productive garden. Mrs. Evans and her daughters were kept busy canning copious amounts of food. One of the first things Mr. Evans did was to hire his neighbours, Gus Johnson and Ole Anderson, expert axemen, to build a large, square-timbered, two-storied house so that the family could live in comfort. It was a work of art. People came from all over to admire the perfection of the beautifully fitted walls and dove-tailed corners.

When Jim Martin had closed his Queenstown store earlier, Charlie Adam, with the help of the ever-faithful Geordie McQuaker, had cleared a few acres of land near the beach on the west side of Charlie's property, about a half mile north of Meta and Trevor, and had built a small store to "test the waters" as he told them. The store did surprisingly well. Encouraged by the progress of this venture, Charlie decided to go after a post office. It was badly needed. A petition was circulated, and he had no trouble in collecting a large number of signatures.

Jackie Williams, born January 27, 1911.
   A lively little boy who kept his parents on their toes.

Charlie Adam, Trevor's neighbour. He had decided to enter the townsite business also, and had a portion of his preemption surveyed into lots and acreages. It was named Graham Centre.

Graham Centre, 1914. Extreme right is the little church. House with "X" built by Sid Wormald for Charlie for five hundred dollars and purchased by Felix Graham. Next to this is the squared-timbered two-and-a-half storey house built by Anderson and Olson which became the store, post office, hotel and library for Graham Centre. Small house in centre was built as a community hall, but taken over by Alex McTavish as his own. Charlie Graham (son of Felix) took this photo and had it made into a postcard. Note the postmark on top right.
Card donated by Sid Wormald

This was Charlie Adam's first cabin, which he built at the Kumdis Narrows. Charlie is in the dark coat and pants. The other man is Cochrane, who lived along the Kumdis River to the east of here. This is where the large Dunroe family stayed until their own preemption house was ready.
Photo—C.M. Adam

St. Luke's Church at Graham Centre was a doll-house of a place. For a bell they used a shake-splitter, which was hit with a piece of iron.
Photo—Sid Wormald

The house that Jim McLay and Jim Allison built on the ridge behind Meta and Trevor. John Boyes, his wife and daughter, Ailo came to live there, to the delight of Meta, as it would be company for her and a playmate for young Jackie.

Left to right: Jim Allison holding Ailo, Meta Williams, Jackie, Jean Greene, wife of Heber Greene, the newly-ordained minister in charge of both the Graham Centre and Port Clements (Queenstown) churches. In the doorway stands Hart Jenkins, Trevor's boyhood friend from Swansea, Jim McLay and Mrs. Boyes.

Photo taken summer of 1914. By summer of 1916 all three men would be dead, killed in battle on the fields of France.

Photo–Rev. H.H.K. Greene

Geordie McQuaker (light sweater) and Charlie Adam wrestle stumps from the new townsite of Graham Centre. Frame house on left is the house Sid Wormald built. On the extreme right is the corner of the squared-timbered building crafted by the expert axemen, Alec Johnson and Ole Anderson of Nadu.
Photo–C.M. Adam

It was a sign of the town's prosperity when Jimmy Campbell opened his newspaper in Masset in 1912. Jimmy stands in shirtsleeves beside Alan Jessup, who sold real estate.
Photo–Mrs. A. Jessup

"I'll need a name before I can apply," he told Trevor. "And after Eli getting turned down on his, I want to make sure I don't run into the same thing. Got any ideas for something original?"

"Well. . . it's almost in the centre of Graham Island," Trevor replied. "How about Graham Centre?" And it was so named.

In the spring of 1912 Charlie was appointed the Inlet's first postmaster. When Eli had gone to the west coast to prospect earlier, he sold his boat, *Queen*, to Charlie as a larger craft and engine was needed for that exposed location. With the awarding of the post office to Graham Centre, Geordie McQuaker was engaged to use the *Queen* to transport mail from New Masset to Graham Centre each week.

In January of 1912 another useful service had been provided for Inlet settlers when Trevor was authorized as a Commissioner For Taking Affidavits and Notary Public. He was kept busy in this capacity from the first day.

Jim McLay and Jim Allison, two of Mayer Lake's preemptors, wanted a house closer to Graham Centre to overnight in occasionally when they came in for groceries and mail. "I've got more land than I'll ever use," Trevor told them. "If you want to pick a small site in behind the timber-licence, you're welcome to put up a place there anytime." The two Jims soon built a nicely-finished storey-and-a-half log house on the bench-land behind the small meadow on the Williams' preemption, close to the trail which ran along the survey line from Queenstown to Graham Centre, marking the timber-licence boundary. (This trail was known locally as the High Trail to distinguish it from the Beach Trail which ran inside the timber near the shoreline from Queenstown to Graham Centre). When friends of McLay and Allison, Mr. and Mrs. John Boyes and small daughter, Ailo, arrived, they were invited by the two men to use the house, with the two Jims overnighting as needed.

Meta was overjoyed to have the Boyes as close neighbours. She got on well with Mrs. Boyes and it would be nice for Jackie to have Ailo to play with. John Boyes and Trevor put in a good trail between the two houses which received plenty of use as the families visited back and forth. Shortly after this another

Mayer Lake preemptor, John McDougall, also obtained permission from Trevor to put up a cabin on the bench for an overnighting place. He built his cabin close to the Boyes.

No doubt it was Trevor's news that McDougall was building a place on the bench which prompted Charlie Adam to confide details of an idea circulating in his tousled head with increasing frequency about that time—sparked in part by the success of his store and post office. "I've had quite a few people asking me for small pieces of land to put cabins on, too," he said. "But we need a proper townsite. Doesn't look as though Tingley is ever going to get anywhere with that project of his. I hear Star Realty is supposed to be putting in some sort of town near Ship Island...across the way there," he gestured towards the mouth of the Inlet. "But that's too far from the main trails, and the anchorage over there is an absolute disaster...so exposed. For that matter, Eli's is not much better. But you take over here—big ships can lie in the lee of Kumdis Island, and if Kumdis Bay is dredged, why we could have a fine, safe, small boat moorage.

"All the main trails around are easy to get to from Graham Centre...the Mexican Tom, Skid Road, Centre Meridian, Mayer Lake, Yakoun River...And when that bridge goes in over Kumdis Narrows they are talking about, well it will feed all the foot traffic from Kumdis Bay and the Slough right through my place."

Adam's main expense in setting up a townsite would be the detailed survey needed to divide his preemption into town-sized lots with a few outlying acreages. Plus the fact that as soon as he registered a townsite he would have to pay taxes on each lot until they were sold. As it stood now, he was only taxed as a homesteader. However, he went to see Fred Nash about undertaking the survey. Nash had so much work lined up it would be late fall of 1912 before he could get round to Adam's project, but he drew up a rough plan for Charlie to show how it might best be laid out. On the strength of this Charlie and Geordie were going to begin clearing and ditching.

The two Scots had already made a large clearing at Charlie's first cabin overlooking the Kumdis Narrows where Charlie had planted a large garden with apple, cherry, oak, and ash trees around the perimeter. Now they began to work like beavers, clearing and stumping the area around the store. This would be the business section of Graham Centre—the hub of which would be another of Gus Johnson and Ole Anderson's masterpieces, a two-storied, square-timbered building. Johnson and Anderson had just finished the last details on the Evans home at the Nadu, and like everyone else who had seen this structure, Charlie was full of admiration.

When the Graham Centre building was completed, the post office, store, and a travelling library were installed downstairs, with plans for the rooms upstairs to be finished off later for a hotel. Charlie and Geordie built a lean-to on the back to serve as living-quarters for themselves. The former store building was enlarged and converted into a home for Geordie's sister, Mrs. Rowan, who with her husband and young son, Willie, were coming from Glasgow to live in Graham Centre. Mrs. Rowan agreed to take in overnight paying guests until the hotel aspect of the store was ready.

There was still activity in Queenstown. Wright and Green had a number of men working for them in connection with the herculean task of transporting eighty-three tons of equipment over the crude road into the Yakoun Valley. This road was commonly called the Skid Road, due to the method of skidding four sleds, each sixty feet long, across horizontal logs laid every so often along the route. The sleds, containing mining equipment and bunk and cookhouses, left Queenstown November 4, 1911, and would take almost a year to reach their destination. To keep the route supplied a crew of men worked in relays, hauling whatever was necessary either on their sturdy backs along the Skid Road or by canoe as far as possible up the log-strewn Yakoun River.

In April of 1912 another drilling company arrived in Queenstown. William Barton's flotilla crossed the Inlet with a sixty-foot scow, powered by an old Stanley Steamer automobile engine, an ex-Vancouver Fire Department boiler, and a propeller cut from some boiler plate. It was laden with supplies and machinery and was followed by several small launches carrying the surplus load. At Queenstown Barton reorganized in preparation for the trip into the Yakoun Valley. He was mystified that Wright and Green had chosen to go overland when they had access to their site by the Yakoun River. This was the way he intended to go. Blasting out the numerous log-jams with funding obtained from the federal Fisheries department (having persuaded them the log-jams hindered fish escapement), Barton worked his way up-river with the barge, using a steam winch to get over any shallow spots. His employers were the Graham Island Collieries.

Charlie Adam may have thought Eli Tingley's dream of a townsite doomed, but he underrated Eli's resiliency. Buoyed up by the coal interests using Queenstown as a base, and knowing that he could at least get a Crown Grant, Eli persuaded brother Bert to become part of the project. Both brothers knew it was now or never to make the move. Eli couldn't afford to wait for clearance with the timber company. If they let Charlie Adam get too far ahead of them, the government goodies such as a wharf, roads, and school would be established in Graham Centre, and Queenstown would have a slim chance as a townsite.

Accommodation was always in short supply in the area, so Bert decided to satisfy this in a bold way. On May 17, 1912, the steamer *Vadso* piloted by her skipper, Captain Nowell, anchored off Queenstown. Over the next three days a small mountain of building supplies was ferried ashore—Bert had brought complete building materials to build a twenty-eight by sixty-foot, two-story, frame-construction hotel, together with most of the furnishings.

"Going to call it the Yakoun Hotel," Eli told Trevor. "He's putting in a big dining room. . .which can double for a dance hall when need be, plus a large kitchen, pantry, good-sized lobby, and a small suite downstairs. Upstairs will be bedrooms and a bathroom. Going to have hot and cold running water in the bathroom, lobby, kitchen, and the suite. This will come from an elevated tank to be filled by pumping from a well. And he's going to add a wing to the hotel for a good-sized store and post office, with living quarters above."

A crew of carpenters under Charles Clayton of Victoria had come with Bert to begin construction immediately. Also on the *Vadso* was Laura, Bert and Eli's sister, and May and Ruth Woods. A third Woods sister, Florence, planned to join them in a few months. The girls had begged to be included in the townsite venture and were such lively company, the boys never regretted for a moment the decision to let them come.

Several tents were soon erected to house the new arrivals, together with tarpaulins to protect the supplies from the weather. A large clearing was made among the trees, despite the fact that they were officially still owned by the Graham Steamship, Coal and Lumber Company.

"Oh, we'll soon get that squared away," Bert said to the dubious. "The worst they can do is charge us for whatever trees we cut down." So the foundations for the hotel and store were soon ready for the carpenters to begin the actual building. Eli and Bert put up a large storage shed at the edge of the beach in front of the hotel site, then built a small dock and float to land supplies and tie up launches. With the shallowness of Stewart Bay to contend with, this dock was to some extent a tidal affair, but very useful.

The weather was excellent during this period, and the ladies, all ardent tennis players, recruited volunteers from the many young bachelors now working on the survey gangs and pack trails to build a tennis court on a patch of clay near the beach east of the hotel. Scraping, clearing, and rolling as they went, willing hands soon made a fast court ready for play. With a six-foot section of a spruce log some four feet in diameter for a roller, the well-patronized court was kept in tip-top condition. Meta, who had been a keen tennis buff in Swansea, was welcomed eagerly and enjoyed the competition with people who came from all around to play on the new court. Delkatla's Charles Wilson was so impressed with the whole idea he built a similar court in his embryo townsite, and before long inter-community tennis matches were being held regularly, extending into community picnics and dances.

On September 30, 1912, there was a gala opening of the new Tingley hotel. Bert had already sent for his widowed mother to come to live with them and had also applied for that sure-fire attraction—a liquor licence. But Mrs. Tingley, a leading member of the Victoria Temperance League, was so aghast at her son's action that Bert deferred to her wishes and cancelled the application. Instead, his advertisements for the Yakoun Hotel stressed that there was "No bar in connection with this establishment."

The hotel's grand opening was a success. Guests came from as far away as Prince Rupert and Victoria to take part in the celebrations, and the entertainment lasted well into the early morning hours—despite the "no bar" rule. Accommodations were stretched to the limit. The Prince Rupert guests were Alfred Carse, E.D. Tite, J.G. Scott, and M.M. Stephens, all of whom made the trip in Mr. Stephens launch. With them was the guest of honour, Herbert S. Clements, MP from Ottawa, from whom Bert and Eli obviously expected great things. And first on the list was a deep-water wharf.

As Eli introduced Mr. Clements to the crowd gathered for the ribbon-cutting, he announced that with the opening of the new hotel a new era was also beginning for Queenstown. To start things off it was to have a new name. "The Honourable Mr. Clements has kindly consented to have his name used, and from now on Queenstown will be known as Port Clements." The Honourable Member, beaming from ear to ear, made the appropriate reply, cut the ribbon, signed the guest book, and the deed was done.

Charlie Adam listened to all of this with apprehension. He also needed a deep-water wharf for Graham Centre to develop and with Trevor's help had taken soundings off the point between their two preemptions. There was deep water at four hundred feet. The wharf which Mr. Clements was expected to deliver for the town which now bore his name would have to go out more than seven hundred feet and could very possibly be adversely affected by the current from the Yakoun River sweeping into the Inlet close by. Charlie prepared his petition for the pier at Graham Centre, marshalling all the advantages of his location—shelter provided by Kumdis Island, clear title to his land, converging trails, and so on, then crossed his fingers that common sense might prevail over politics when Ottawa made the decision.

"It was a damned good letter," Trevor told Meta after Charlie had called him into the store to read it. "But no doubt

Herbert S. Clements, MP, for whom, on September 30, 1912, Eli Tingley
named his townsite, Port Clements.
Photo–W.J. Topley, National Archives of Canada.

Frank Lennie Donroe and his wife with seven of their ten children. *Left to right*: Annie, Jim, Cecile, Joseph, Barney, Patrick and Helen. Missing from the photo are Mary, Josephine and Rose.
Photo—L. Rennie

it will all depend on how influential Herbert Clements is in Ottawa. There'll only be one wharf go in—that's certain. If it does go at Port Clements, Charlie will be out of luck for his place." The Williams' were doing their best to keep neutral in the dispute, situated as they were between the two townsites and on friendly terms with all participants.

Much of Trevor's income derived from his "letter writing" as he called it. He was in demand to sign papers, deal with snags in applications, and contact the numerous governmental departments regarding the endless problems besetting a new situation and people new to the procedures. His office background and experience gained as secretary of the Settlers Association had given him a great deal of information in this field, and at times he had more work than he could handle. But he still took advantage of any outdoor activity to earn a few dollars, such as working on trails in the vicinity, if there was a shortage of applicants for a particular job.

In January of 1913 Fred Nash completed the detailed survey of Graham Centre. Charlie still had to wait for the provincial government to select its usual quarter of the town-sized lots before he could register it, but he was free to sell the outlying acreages and did. At the same time he set about erecting more buildings in the townsite proper. Sid Wormald, who had a preemption behind the timber licence line which ran along Kumdis Slough, agreed to build a two-story frame house near the store. This was soon purchased by Felix Graham, an accountant with Wright and Green. Graham, with his wife and son, Charles, came to the Centre to live. Adam persuaded Sid to accept an acreage fronting the sandy bay north of the townsite in lieu of the $500 he had promised him for building the house.

Felix Graham's boss, Frank Wright, bought an acreage from Charlie near Sid Wormald's and hired young Bill Rennie from Mayer Lake to build him a house. The Wrights were toying with the idea of a lodge eventually, hoping to entice sightseers from the mainland who would be shown the beauties of the area. Bill Rennie liked Graham Centre better than his site at Mayer Lake, so he bought an acreage north of Wormald and built a small frame house so that his bride could move with him from Mayer Lake. Their daughter, Dorothy, born in December of 1913, was the first baby born in Graham Centre. Anne Adam, Charlie's sister, came to keep house for her hard-working brother and so entranced entrepreneur Alex McTavish, that before long Alex also built a house in Graham Centre. Arthur Richardson and Thomas O'Callaghan bought property, as did the O'Flynns. The O'Flynns agreed to run the hotel upstairs in the Graham Centre store. Grandpa Godwin, who with his widower son had preempted land next to Sid Wormald behind the timber-licence in Kumdis Slough, thought preemption life too isolated for his teen-aged granddaughter, Mabel, and bought acreage from Charlie which faced Kumdis Bay.

"Never seen such good soil in my life," he told Meta in the store one day. "Everything is huge. Lettuce, carrots, spuds—and my scarlet runner beans are up one side of the house and down over the other. Mabel's daisies are as big as saucers. Wonderful place!"

With so many young adults in the general area and the vitality of this group needing a stimulating diversion from the work of pioneering, an interesting social life developed. A lively debating society provided many hours of strenuous mental activity when the people of Graham Centre took on the folks from Port Clements. The tennis court was in full swing when weather permitted, and Eli and Bert scooped out a depression ready for a skating pond in winter. The travelling library in Adam's store frequently had more patrons than books it was so well used. Borrowers came from Mayer Lake, Kumdis, Graham Centre, Sewall, and the Yakoun as well as Port Clements, with lengthy discussions taking place in the store when the books were exchanged. A Settlers League, Farmers Institute, and Conservative Association drew active members from all the communities in the Masset and Masset Inlet areas, and there was a good deal of inter-community fellowship despite the strenuous competition between various townsite promoters vying for prospective residents.

In the spring of 1913 the Star Realty Company put their townsite near Ship Island on the market, naming it Sewall after Samuel Dart Sewall, a member of the company, who lived there with his wife. The Seventh Day Adventist group who built a small mill at Sewall in 1912 had moved shortly after to live at Watun River. But they continued active operation of the mill in Sewall for several years.

One thing the Masset Inlet communities lacked was a school. And with families now arriving with children, that became a priority. "Trouble is," Trevor said to Meta, "it's the old chicken and egg story. You can't get a school until you have enough kids to make up the required number,and you can't get families with children until you have a school." It appeared a solution to this problem was at hand when Frank Lennie Le Tonturier Donroe, his wife, and ten children came to live in Sewall. Not only did Donroe have enough children in his own family to qualify for a school, but he was a registered teacher. Mr. Donroe was looking for the cheap land "ready for the plough" he had read about in the government brochures. But with the prices being asked for land at Sewall he realized he wouldn't find what he wanted there.

He hired Charlie Adam to take him and his brood to Kumdis Bay where he had heard there might be good preemption land available. They would camp in the woods until they found a place, he told Charlie. The idea of all those children and their mother going out into the forest without any kind of shelter was appalling to Charlie, and he offered Donroe the use of his Kumdis Narrows cabin until a better arrangement could be made.

"Och, Charlie," begged Mrs. Rowan when she heard this news. "Could ye no give Mr. Donroe a wee bitty land in Graham Centre and get him to set up a school here? The man plainly has no money, and he would be too proud to live for long on land not his own. We have to send our Willie to school, and there's others in the same situation who would come here to live if only there was a school. Take Crosses and Hasties at Mayer Lake. They've had to go to Masset so their young ones can get schooled. They would far rather be up here nearer their menfolk. . . ."

Charlie interrupted her. "That Donroe. He's not wanting any town. He'll only stay until he can find land to preempt."

"Aye," replied Mrs. Rowan. "But if we could just get a

school started, then should he leave . . . surely the government would send another teacher if we can get enough families to come here with children. Without a school you'll never get them," she warned. But Charlie was adamant. Lending his cabin was one thing, but if Donroe took land in his townsite he would have to pay the same as everyone else. "Not fair to other people," he told her and nothing she could say would persuade him to make an exception in Donroe's case.

Donroe did find preemptable land about a mile or so inland from Kumdis Bay, and sending his two oldest sons (the elder barely eighteen) to build a rough cabin, Donroe took his family into the woods. Being the only licenced teacher available for them, he sought and obtained a government stipend to teach—holding classes in his own cabin. Mrs. Rowan groaned in anguish over Charlie's shortsightedness. She pleaded with her brother Geordie to intercede. But Geordie said he would not interfere with Charlie's decisions. Graham Centre was not to have such an opportunity again.

It was one in a series of events which was inexorably to doom Graham Centre's development into Masset Inlet's leading townsite despite its promising start and apparent advantages over its rivals, Sewall and Port Clements. The bridge which everyone thought would be built at Kumdis Narrows had unexpected opposition. Ed O'Brian suddenly acquired an old sailboat and claimed that any bridge at the Narrows would block his right of access via navigable waters to his established homesite further up. He was successful in having the location of the bridge changed from the Narrows, where it was really needed, to the Kumdis River—a mile away from this site. In fact the new location was in the middle of nowhere at that time. None of the main trails led to it. O'Brian had hacked out a crude set of blazes into Port Clements, but it is doubtful if he ever used this route.

The local uproar from the Kumdis area was soothed by a government spokesman saying that new trails would be put in to connect the old ones with the bridge and Graham Centre. However, there was enough political influence in Port Clements to see that this did not happen. Instead, the new trails led directly to the bridge and into Port Clements,

completely by-passing Graham Centre. Once the bridge was a
fact, O'Brian sold his boat.

Then came the news that Eli had received official
confirmation from the timber company that they were
prepared to sign a quit claim regarding the trees they owned
on Tingley's townsite. Eli would have to pay their price, but
he had already arranged financing for this, and it was only a
question of months before he would finally be free of this
long-standing obstruction. The veteran surveyor, Fred Nash,
came to do the townsite survey. Nash was becoming an expert
in this field now, having laid out Delkatla, Sewall, and Graham
Centre townsites. He completed the Port Clements survey in
April of 1913.

The big Irish parson, Reverend William Hogan, had
managed a few trips to the Inlet to hold services in the dining
room of Tingley's Yakoun Hotel, but his duties at the two
Massets were really all he could handle. One of the Port
Clements residents, Albert R. Mallory, arranged for Reverend
Len Bygraves, the Presbyterian minister in Queen Charlotte
City, to come to Port Clements on a regular basis. Mr.
Bygraves' popularity and well-attended services were viewed
with apprehension in the mainland Church of England
headquarters. They regarded the north end of Graham Island
as their exclusive territory and decided to post a resident parson to the Masset Inlet area and nip the competition in the
bud.

Eli, hearing of this, suggested that any newly-appointed
Masset Inlet clergyman make his headquarters in Port
Clements, and offered to donate a lot for a combined church
and rectory, adding that until the building was ready he would
be pleased to make the guest house at the head of Stewart Bay
available for the new minister. The Bishop in Prince Rupert
accepted Eli's offer and sent young Heber Greene to be the
Inlet's first resident preacher. Heber, a recent graduate of the
University of Toronto and Wycliffe College, brought his bride,
Jean, to the rough frontier cabin and began his pastoral career.
Shortly after arriving he was formally ordained in the Old
Masset Church with Bishop du Vernet and Rev. William
Hogan conducting the service. Anne Adam urged her brother

to donate a lot in Graham Centre to the Anglicans for a church also.

St. Luke's was the name given to the sixteen by twenty-foot Graham Centre church built by Sid Wormald and Jim Shaw of the Kumdis Slough. It was a doll-house of a place. The hand-hewn pews and lectern, the home-made altar covered with one of Anne Adam's fine linen tablecloths and adorned with silver candlesticks from someone else's trunk, bespoke a community church with many willing volunteers to keep it functioning. Someone made sure there was plenty of firewood for the heater, while somebody else saw to it that the fire was lit in ample time to make the small building comfortably warm for the weekly service. The place was kept dusted and polished, with fresh flowers for altar and window sills during the summer. A large vase of wilderness shrubbery on the floor by the small portable organ brightened winter days.

Like other churches operated by the Church of England in isolated regions at that time, St. Luke's was run on non-denominational lines so that people from all branches of the Protestant faith felt at ease. As Heber Greene was to say later, "Thank goodness this was the case, for if I'd had to depend on Anglicans to fill the pews, I'd probably have been preaching just to Jean on some Sundays." As it was, every seat would be taken, and often chairs had to be brought in to take care of the overflow. Meta, a devout Welsh Congregationalist, agreed to be the organist for the little foot-pumped organ to accompany the singing of old and familiar hymns. Everyone, dressed in Sunday best, would rise and belt out with gusto and vigour the verses, so that the entire Graham Centre clearing fairly echoed with music.

"The bell for St. Luke's is singularly appropriate for a pioneer church," Heber Greene wrote his bishop. "They have a shake-splitter hung on a wire which is hit with a piece of iron!"

Meanwhile, the Port Clements church was already in operation, Heber having officiated at the first service there on January 25, 1913. Named St. Mark's, it was slightly larger than the one in Graham Centre as its twenty-two by thirty-six feet included an annex for living quarters for the Greenes.

The Anglicans had made a fortunate choice in Heber Greene. Honest and forthright, he cared little if those he helped were "ours" or "theirs," and during his stay on the Charlottes he made his churches the hub of their particular community. In addition to Graham Centre and Port Clements, he also regularly held services at Sewall, Tlell, mining camps in the Yakoun Valley, and, upon invitation, walked many times to the south end of the Island to hold services.

Both Bert and Eli were keenly aware of the need for a school if they hoped to attract families to their townsite. No Donroe with his ready-made class had landed on their doorstep, but they did have a first-rate teacher in their sister, Laura, and like Mrs. Rowan of Graham Centre, they were sure the Hastie and Cross families, who between them had six school-aged children, could be induced to move to an Inlet settlement with the right proposition.

Eli offered them land in Port Clements at what he called his "promotional prices"—almost gratis. Since the Crosses had a cow, pigs, and chickens, they would need an acreage, and Eli gave them a site near the end of the Mexican Tom Trail, then organized a work-bee to help put up a family-sized log home. Bill Hastie, Walter Cross's brother-in-law, wanted to put up a recreation building containing a poolroom and dance hall as well as a possible bakery—in addition to a home for his family. Eli offered him lots near Martin's store. With enough children in the area now for a school, Eli donated the use of his original cabin, and in June of 1913 Laura Tingley held the first class in Port Clements.

Charlie Adam didn't need Mrs. Rowan to tell him after this how much he had erred with Donroe. It became all too plain. With land available and a school opened for their children, families flocked to Port Clements—houses springing up all over the place as soon as the townsite was cleared.

Perhaps the best barometer for Port Clements' future was the reopening and enlarging by James Martin of his former store and the hiring of Francis Evans from the Nadu as a full-time clerk. But particularly satisfying was the purchase of lots from Eli by his long-time rival, Charles Harrison of

Masset. Harrison, who never lost a chance to belittle the place, nevertheless couldn't resist the opportunity to speculate and had two frame houses built in Port Clements as a business venture. Jimmy Campbell, editor of the *Queen Charlotte Islander,* moved his operation from Queen Charlotte City into an office-cum-residence that Eli built for him near Martin's store. "It's the coming place," Jimmy told a dismayed Windy Young who tried hard to dissuade him.

And as hoped, MP Herbert S. Clements came through for Eli. The government chose the townsite bearing Mr. Clements' name as the location for a wharf.

Drilling operations in the Yakoun Valley had come to a temporary halt by 1913. Wright and Green's company, which had utilized the Skid Road, had run out of funds at the end of 1912. In fact Mr. and Mrs. Green left in a great hurry to avoid the angry recipients of bad cheques issued by the company. Wright, not involved in the financial end of the company, was better able to weather the fiasco. He remained and worked for awhile for Barton as a driller. Barton's contract with the Graham Island Collieries expired in the late spring of 1913, and with the demand for lumber in Port Clements created by all the building, plus the new wharf, Barton decided to capitalize on the bonanza. He needed waterfront property, so Eli suggested a site near the popular tennis court—but was to rue that decision as before long the waste from the mill completely obliterated the fine clay court.

"Great news," Trevor told Meta in that same year of 1913. "Eli has gone to Victoria to get married! He and Ruth Woods are tying the knot next weekweek then coming back here to live...there's going to be a big celebration to welcome them when they arrive." Ruth had always been at Eli's side in her own quiet way—to agonize with him over set-backs and rejoice with news of any progress. Bert was the practical business head, and no doubt it was Bert who really kept the project on course. But it was Ruth who was the soulmate, who understood the dream and how much it meant to Eli to bring it to fruition.

There was still considerable activity in Graham Centre during 1913 despite the progress of Port Clements. Adam and

Geordie put in a slipway and float in March and were soon swamped with boats in for repairs. People in the area still had to come to Graham Centre for mail and postal service, and the travelling library was as popular as ever. Card games and dances were held in McTavish's Hall, a building erected by volunteers to be a church and community hall but taken over by the silver-tongued McTavish as his own. And Charlie Adam continued to receive many inquiries about land in Graham Centre by prospective buyers.

"Trouble is," Trevor commented to Meta, "he's asking such steep prices for his lots he's scaring people off—especially now that they hear Eli's lots are soon coming on the market. With Bert handling the business end of that, you may be sure he'll see to it that their prices will undercut Charlie's significantly, for the first while at least. Although how Eli expects to recoup enough money to foot that whopping bill from the timber company...heaven only knows. Anyhow, it doesn't matter to us which town goes ahead, we're pretty well in the middle here...and they are all such damned fine neighbours, can't really take any sides in the affair."

Meta nodded in agreement, then asked Trevor to see about making their backyard more secure. Young Jackie was showing increased curiosity about the environment beyond the confines of the fenced area, and Meta had noticed his ability to climb was becoming pretty proficient. Together they went out to see what could be done, and Meta's worst fears were realized. Their small son was nowhere in sight.

"Oh my God!..." Trevor was out of the gate in a flash, racing to the beach. Then to the larger garden in the back. Meta ran to the creek where they got their water. No sign.

"You look around the chicken-house and meadow," called Trevor "and I'll go to Boyes. Maybe he's gone to play with Ailo." Trevor sped along the trail calling the little boy's name. No answer. And he was not at Boyes. John Boyes and the two Jims were just finishing a mid-morning cup of tea and immediately joined in the search—all adults keenly aware of how quickly one can become lost in the woods. And there was another forest danger they hardly dared mention. When large trees are blown over during high winds, the roots are yanked out as they fall, taking great amounts of soil with them and leaving a depression, sometimes several feet deep. These fill with water—a lethal situation for a toddler.

They fanned out. Two took the top end of the meadow where they saw Meta coming across, still in slippers and apron. There was just no sign anywhere. It was time to go to Graham Centre for more help. Trevor fled along the trail. Taking the steps into the store three at a time, he burst through the open door and then nearly collapsed with relief.

Jackie sat on the counter greedily stuffing iced cookies into his mouth, watched by a beaming Charlie Adam. "He wandered in here about a half hour ago," Charlie told the breathless father. "I wondered why he was on his own... thought you must be outside talking to someone." Charlie had been in the habit of giving the little boy a cookie each time his parents brought him into the store, and no doubt it was the lure of this treat which had given impetus to the lad's choice of destination once he was out on his own.

It was shortly after this that the telephone lines connecting most of the communities on Graham Island were installed, including a link to join Graham Centre to Port Clements. The line ran past the Williams' house, so they were hooked in—a life-saver in case of emergency. This was the typical rural line of that day. The subscribers were on one long party line and called each other by a series of rings, such as one short and two long, or two short and two long, and so on. If you lived between Port Clements and Masset you could ring anyone on that line. If you wished to speak to someone—say at Tow Hill—you would call the Masset operator who would have to put you through using the series of rings which applied to the Masset to Tow Hill line. This meant that each time someone on your party line was called, the phones on all that line rang. But you soon got used to your own set of rings and could pick them out almost without consciously listening. The ringing was done by cranking a small handle on the side of the phone.

In the fall of 1913 a familiar face appeared at the Williams' door late one afternoon. Trevor could hardly believe what he saw. It was the tall form of his boyhood friend, Hart Jenkins from Swansea. "Heard so much about your doings out here in

Canada from your father and Gwilym, I thought I'd come and
see what it was all about," he explained as Trevor pumped his
hand and hugged him in a warm welcome. "Come in my lad,"
the visitor was told. "Stay as long as you like. We'd love to
have you."

Within a few days it was apparent that Hart was entertaining
the idea of becoming a homesteader himself, hoping to find
land near Trevor. It was equally obvious that any such plan
would be courting disaster. "He's an absolute prince of a fellow," Trevor told Meta, "but he has to be one of the most
hopeless chaps on his own I've ever seen. I wouldn't dare let
him into the woods by himself. He'd be lost in five minutes. I'd
like to put up a small cabin for him beside us and persuade him
to stay here. What do you think?" Meta liked Hart as much as
Trevor did, so it was fine with her. His good company would
more than compensate for any inconvenience.

In no time Hart was like one of the family, going to all the
community events with them, lending a hand with the mun-
dane chores of wood-cutting, gardening, and so forth, and
particularly enjoying the hunting and fishing trips Trevor took
him on in the Linton boat.

"No wonder you love it, Trevor," he said. "Its better than
any of the posh estates back home, and here it is. . .all yours.
What a glorious life!"

TWELVE

AS 1913 TURNED THE CORNER into 1914, life in the pioneer settlements was a satisfying experience with promise of a rewarding future. There appeared to be plenty of work in the various aspects of developing the communities, the building of government roads, trails, and bridges and maintenance of telephone lines, wharves, and floats. Coal activity in the Yakoun Valley required a constant crew of packers, suppliers, and workers and there was always work to be had with the survey parties—an activity which seemed to go on perpetually. But perhaps it was the community life and good fellowship which lifted hearts most of all. Socializing was engaged in at any excuse, and people seemed to really care about one another's well-being.

Typical was the Christmas dinner of 1913 when the ladies of Graham Centre held a community dinner for all the bachelors of the area—and anyone else wanting companionship at that special time of year. Forty people sat down to loaded tables, and with Alex McTavish in full form as the master of ceremonies, there was plenty of lively entertainment and jovial singing afterwards. As was the custom, children were welcomed, then as the evening wore on they were put to sleep on coats, benches, or chairs until their parents were ready to go home.

A week later, on New Year's Eve, Bill Hastie opened his new dance hall in Port Clements with a big masquerade ball. Hastie sent his gas-boat to Graham Centre to pick up a load and took them all back again around 5 a.m. when the dance was pretty well over. With Meta leading the way holding the lantern, Trevor and Hart took turns carrying the sleeping Jackie along the trail from Graham Centre to their home.

The Star Realty town of Sewall had attracted some seventy people to its environs, and they, too, took part in the inter-community events, as did the Nadu homesteaders, now numbering eighteen along the road which ran inland for two miles. Pioneering preemptors from the Yakoun, Centre Meridian, and Kumdis areas were also much in evidence.

Watun River, sometimes known as the "Holy City" because of the two church groups (the Seventh Day Adventists and the Roman Catholics) making headquarters there, was becoming a busy settlement with the two churches, store, post office, hotel, bakery and a boat-yard which produced several excellently built small launches. In 1914 even a school was opened at Watun (locally called Woden), indicating that families with children were making this place home as well as the young bachelors more commonly found in the beginning of a pioneer era. On March 19, 1914, Port Clements at last became an officially registered townsite, and a post office was granted. Bert made room for it in the annex to his hotel, and Albert R. Mallory was appointed postmaster. It seemed as though nothing could halt Eli's vision of a town now. And in Graham Centre there was also a rosy outlook. Frank Wright, who had earlier hinted about putting in a lodge, now formally announced that he was making arrangements to build a large holiday hotel in the Centre for visitors from the mainland. This would mean a wide variety of jobs in the form of staffing, guides, and launch operators to make sure the guests were well-looked after. Charlie Adam rubbed his hands in glee as he told Trevor the news. "We're away and running now. This is going to be the making of the place."

But the murder on June 28th, 1914, of a little-known Austrian prince thousands of miles away was to change everyone's dreams.

Actually, when the newspapers arrived from the mainland early in July describing the assassination of Franz Ferdinand and his wife in the Austrian border town of Sarajevo, little attention was paid to the item. It rated as interesting, but certainly not earth-shaking. Readers were told that a hot-headed member of the Serbian Black Hands had shot the couple as they drove along a quiet street. There was an added note explaining that the Black Hands was an organization attempting to create a great Slavic state at the expense of the Austro-Hungarian Empire.

Subsequent newspapers contained reports that the Austrians, irritated by the activities of the Black Hands and furious over the assassination of their Crown Prince and his wife, had decided to use the incident to discipline their troublesome neighbours. Instead of merely arresting the murderer, they drew up a set of hard conditions, complete with an ultimatum: if the Serbians didn't comply immediately, Austria would declare war. Serbia did refuse to meet the conditions, and on July 28th, a month after the assassination, Austria formally declared war. Now the headlines were in bold black type. However the general reaction was "Tempest in a teapot."

But the dominoes had begun to tumble. Russia, taking umbrage at the threat to her Slavic protege, began mobilizing. Germany, an ally of Austria, warned Russia ". . . mobilization means war." And again the headlines screamed in alarm. Russia ignored Germany's warning. Now France, allied to Russia, and still smoldering over the loss to Germany in 1871 of the Alsace-Lorraine provinces following the Franco-Prussian war, reacted against Germany, saying she would back Russia. The swaggering German Kaiser promptly declared war on both of them.

This meant that Germany would have to fight two wars: against France in the west and Russia in the east. The Germans decided to defeat France quickly, then turn around and overcome Russia. The fastest way into France was through Belgium. However Britain, France, and Germany had all guaranteed Belgium neutrality. German war lords decided a violation of Belgium was a military necessity. Belgium wouldn't put up much resistance, they thought, and Britain would not be so foolish as to enter a war merely to fulfill a promise. They were wrong on both counts.

The invasion of Belgium by Germany began on August 3, 1914, and at midnight the following day Britain declared war on Germany.

At this crucial time, with world events precipitating towards disaster, the north end of the Queen Charlottes suddenly suffered an agonizing news blackout. The *Prince Albert*, which regularly brought mail and papers to the area, was out of commission from the end of July until the third week in September. She had run on rocks near Prince Rupert, and no replacement was sent to take her place during repairs.

And, after the electrifying announcement that a world war was imminent, all telephone and telegraph services to the Charlottes were ordered to stop lest messages be intercepted by a German cruiser reported somewhere in the Pacific. It seemed impossible to get any verified information.

In mid-August a group of men needing to go to the mainland on urgent business chartered Andy McCrea's *Westover*. Andy's return was eagerly awaited. The news he brought back was not good. All public and private projects were closing down until war was over—in fact unemployment was already rife on the mainland. Andy had also heard the disquieting rumour that coastal shipping was to be discontinued for the duration, in case enemy ships obtained vital information from wireless messages sent by steamers as they moved from one small settlement to another.

When the *Albert* eventually resumed her run, newspaper and magazine accounts of what had transpired during the interim only seemed to add to the apprehension and confusion. With so much uncertainty Trevor decided to go to Prince Rupert himself and get some facts so that he and Meta could plan the best course of action in this emergency. He left on the *Albert* the first week in October. Hart Jenkins went with him—but Hart was in no doubt whatsoever what he was going to do. The recruiting office was his destination. "You should have seen him," Trevor told Meta later. "He put on his full-dress Dragoon uniform, all smartly pressed, boots polished and the lot. Bounded up the steps of the recruiting office, saluted smartly and announced 'Captain Hart Jenkins reporting for duty, sir.' The officer in charge was open-mouthed in astonishment. Hart's professionalism stood out like a shining light in all that straggling line of volunteers. The brass came out and welcomed him with open arms, and he was shipped off to the main depot in Victoria immediately."

"I'll probably follow you shortly," Trevor told Hart as they parted. "But I owe it to Meta to have a look at all possibilities first."

The economic future on the mainland was every bit as uncertain as it appeared on the Charlottes, and the general impression was that until the war was over, things were not going to improve. In fact, they could only get worse. Germany, although acknowledged to be far better prepared for war than Britain or her allies, was regarded as a country-bumpkin, easily put to rout if everyone pitched in before the boastful Kaiser had a chance to gain too much momentum.

The Belgians were reported to be putting up an unexpectedly stiff resistance and at one point had almost turned the invaders back, despite overwhelming odds. But it was only a temporary gain, and they were going to need a tremendous amount of assistance. It was generally agreed that with a good response to the recruiting call, the war would be over within a year, then everyone could get on with their lives.

Meta had told Trevor he must do whatever he felt best, and she would go along with his decision—but it was an anxious and fearful wait. Like most wives, she couldn't bear to think of him going off to war. "Please, dear Lord," she prayed, "let there be some other solution."

Certainly the last thing Trevor wanted to do was become involved in another war. His memories of the South African campaign were still too vivid. But after weighing all aspects he came to the conclusion it was the only action one could decently take under the circumstances. He didn't think he could properly live with himself if he let others do the fighting so that he could live in peace. And so in the second week of October, 1914, Trevor enlisted as a private in the 68th

Regiment, Prince Rupert Light Infantry, Overseas Company, and received permission to return to the Charlottes before assuming duty in a couple of weeks.

It had taken much soul-searching, and even after the decision had been made, the thirty-four-year-old man felt misgivings. "Damn! Well...it is done now," he thought. "Let's hope it will soon be over..." There really wasn't any other choice he could have made.

Meta, despite her prayers, knew this would be Trevor's decision, but her anxiety now became even more stressful. Added to the worry of Trevor being in the terrible battles now being described in the papers was her own decision to keep as close to him as she could. In apprehension of boat travel at the best of times, she nevertheless refused to even consider remaining on the west coast of British Columbia if her Trevor had to go to war on the other side of the Atlantic. She would take Jackie, now three and a half, and return to her people in Swansea. At least there she could see him whenever he had leave. Somehow she would endure the wild malevolence of Hecate Strait in early winter and the gales of the Atlantic—ordeals she just had to put out of her mind. Fortunately, there was so much to do in closing up their log home for an extended period, she could concentrate on the immediate necessities and block everything else out.

"Just take the barest items of personal clothing and toiletries," Trevor suggested. "That will be plenty for you to look after with young Jackie. You can get anything else you need when you arrive in Swansea." So they left the comfortably furnished home intact, ready for their return. Charlie Adam agreed to keep an eye on the place and was given the key. It was the first time their house had ever had a lock on the door.

They had less than two weeks to make arrangements; secure the house and outbuildings against winter storms; dispose of the chickens; and sell the cherished Linton boat which had played such a significant role in Trevor's early pioneering years. Then a whirlwind of goodbyes. An exhausting time physically and emotionally.

There were many familiar faces on the *Albert* when they

went on board. Scores of young men from the area had made the same decision, and most had done just as the Williams'—left their cabins and, with little more than a change of clothes, were on their way to get the war over with so that they could get back to the life they found so satisfying—pioneering on a western frontier.

As the dim outline of Rose Spit buoy faded into the haze of sea spray and rain, Trevor could feel the familiar pitch and roll of the *Albert* as she accepted the challenge of Hecate Strait. It had all the characteristics of another stormy trip. He left his place at the rail and, lurching along, descended a companionway to the ship's saloon. As he passed the purser's office several men were listening to war news just being relayed by the wireless. The British battleship *Audacious* had been sunk by a German mine off Northern Ireland. "Damn bastards!" exclaimed one officer. "They are getting too close. It was only a week ago that one of their U-boats torpedoed the cruiser *Hawke*, and they say that U-Boats have been spotted in Scapa Flow and Loch Ewe." The purser broke in to say that it had now been confirmed that the three British cruisers, *Aboukir*, *Cressy* and *Hogue*, had been torpedoed within a space of one hour on the 22nd of September with a loss of fourteen hundred sailors. Grim news indeed. The *Hogue* had stopped to pick up survivors from the *Aboukir* and *Cressy* when she was hit.

"Well at least," thought Trevor, "it looks as though the Germans are only going after naval vessels." But it was small comfort. They were operating all too close to waters Meta and Jackie would pass through.

Cautiously opening their stateroom door he found Meta lying on the lower berth beside a sleeping Jackie. She raised a finger to her lips, "Shh..."

He nodded an understanding. Hecate Strait was enough to cope with for the moment. Climbing into the upper berth he gradually relaxed. It would be at least five or six hours before they were out of the worst of the seas and into the shelter of the islands off the mainland. This might be the last time the three of them would be together for who knew how long. He would savour these hours...

THIRTEEN

THEIR PARTING AT THE Prince Rupert train depot was so emotional that Trevor completely forgot to give Meta her reams of tickets for the transcontinental train trip and the steamer to Liverpool. These were discovered in his pocket a good half-hour after the train left. "Oh, Migawd!" He rushed to the Grand Trunk Pacific office in alarm. The ticket office personnel were helpfulness personified. Conductors were wired en route to Winnipeg to pass Meta along. There she would receive a new batch of tickets to take her to Montreal where she would get more to cross the Atlantic.

Meanwhile on the train, Meta, in settling young Jackie down for the long trip, discovered Nellie Hammond was on board. Nellie and Jim Hammond had been Tow Hill pioneers in 1912 and, after the birth of their son Harold late that same year, had moved to live in Masset. She, too, had become very friendly with Mrs. Harrison, and this was where Meta first met her. "Jim went to work in Anyox a few months ago," Nellie told Meta. "So Harold and I have been staying in Prince Rupert. When the war broke out Jim wanted to enlist so badly, I had to go along with it. Now Harold and I are on our way to England, to my parents in Folkestone." The two women, delighted to know they would be travelling companions all the way to Britain, were in the midst of their rejoicing when the conductor came for their tickets. And Meta discovered she didn't have any. "They are still in my husband's pocket! Whatever can I do?" Her obvious sincerity and distress convinced the conductor that she was most certainly telling the truth. "Don't you worry, Ma'am," he soothed, "as soon as they get hold of your husband they'll wire new ones, I expect. You just stay put, and we'll get it sorted out."

Meta had kept a reasonably firm handle on her emotions to this point, but the tearful parting from Trevor and now the missing tickets threatened her control. The past month's events began catching up with her, demanding their due. Her stomach had been in such a knot of apprehension and dread for so many weeks she had only coped by resolutely refusing to deal with anything except bare, basic needs. The knowledge that Trevor was going into another war was so scary she could hardly bear it. He had come through the Boer War unscathed when so many of the young men they had both known had lost their lives, but to go into another one now was surely tempting fate. Despite her hopes that some other conclusion might have been found to the dilemma facing them, she had known and understood the "why" of his action. With Hart Jenkins so full of patriotic zeal, to say nothing of McLay and Allison and the other young men they knew talking about enlisting, his decision was inevitable. He couldn't have lived with himself thinking he was letting the others fight a war on his behalf.

By the time she and Jackie had boarded the train on November 4th, some of the European war news was filtering through to the Canadian newspapers. They learned of the gory battle in France between the French and the Germans on the Marne, outside Paris, and the terrible losses near the end of October when the first British volunteers met the Germans at Ypres. "A Bloody Hell. Enormous Casualties," blazed the headlines. Britain was supreme on the sea, it was said, nevertheless the German U-boats seemed to be taking a toll almost at will. And while thinking about the U-Boats came the "what if's" Meta had so desperately been trying to avoid.

Had she done the fair thing to bring Jackie on a trip like this? She knew now that U-boats were active in the North Atlantic as well as elsewhere. If she had stayed in Graham Centre at least they would have been physically safe, but because she couldn't bear the thought of Trevor so far away, she'd had to narrow the distance. Dear God! What if their ship was torpedoed in that icy water? How could she protect Jackie? What if she drowned and he didn't? Who would know who he was? The worry over this became a torment, but at least it provided something constructive for her to do. All the way across the continent her nimble fingers busily embroidered name-tags for every item of Jackie's clothing to say who he was and where he should be sent should the worst happen.

Nellie Hammond was suffering the same mental anguish, so it was a help to be able to talk to one another about their fears. However, the journey across the stormy Atlantic was a nightmare of anticipation. Expecting the thud of a torpedo at any moment, Meta scarcely closed her eyes, and by the time they docked in Liverpool she was completely exhausted from the constant emotional strain. Her brother Jack met her and was totally shocked by her appearance. "You're a wreck, Luv," he said. "Looks like you haven't slept in months."

"I don't think I have," she sobbed, collapsing in his arms.

Trevor's first letter arrived in Swansea remarkably quickly considering war-time conditions. His group had been shipped to Victoria on November 6th, two days after Meta left on the train. They were now part of "B" Company, 30th Battalion, Canadian Expeditionary Force, Willows Camp, Victoria, BC.

"There are plenty of familiar faces here," he wrote. "Alan Jessup, Fred Batchelor, Bert and Ernie Wearmouth, the Metcalfe brothers, Entwistles, Halroyd, Dodgson and his cousin, Reg Partridge (these two had cabins a few miles out along the Mexican Tom Trail), and Smith from Masset, Jim Hammond, and D.M McKay, the land surveyor we knew, just to mention a few.

"For poor McKay," he added, "it is a rough initiation. We all sleep in rows on blankets on the wooden floor, and each night at lights out McKay kneels and says his prayers. Takes some courage in this collection, believe me. And every night our sergeant, a tough professional soldier invaluable for his military knowledge, will come in staggering drunk from the sergeant's mess to fall on his blankets which are beside me. Never seems to interfere with his duties next morning, but absolutely outrages McKay, who moans and groans at the thought of this lost soul who may soon lose his life in action. His sorrow does not perturb the good sergeant—nor me for that matter. I remember too well old soldiers' habits in the Boer War."

It was about mid-December when Trevor heard about a privately funded group acting for the Executive Committee of the Welsh Army Corps. They wanted to send a squad of twenty Welshmen from Vancouver directly to Wales to join the Welsh Army Corps, and they were particularly interested in anyone with previous military experience. Curious, Trevor went for an interview with a Mr. R. Marpole early in January. Marpole, an executive assistant in the office of the Canadian Pacific Railroad, was making all arrangements and explained that it was a simple matter to obtain a discharge from the Canadian Expeditionary Force in order to transfer to another branch of the Allied military. "I would really like to include you in the group," he said to Trevor after the interview. "With your qualifications I would place you in charge of the squad, and I honestly believe you would be in line for a commission once you join the Welsh Army. . . we certainly would do all we could for you in this respect. There will be nineteen men and yourself going from Vancouver to Liverpool."

On January 12, 1915, Trevor received a letter to confirm the conditions. Mr. Marpole wrote, "I have arranged the necessary rail and steamer accommodation through to Liverpool and Llandudno. You will all go tourist coach from Vancouver to St. John, leaving January 21st. From St. John to Liverpool it will be by second-class cabin on the *Grampian* and all arrangements will be made for quick dispatch to Llandudno at Liverpool. I agree to pay the fares and meals of the men through to Llandudno. I also agree to do the same from Liverpool to Vancouver on the return journey, provided each individual carries out the declaration made by him on Attestation, or if incapacitated by injury when in regular service of the Welsh Army Corps. You will be given three weeks between the time of your arrival in Llandudno and the date of your enrollment with the Welsh Army as requested. You should secure your release from the Canadian Militia immediately."

On January 18th, Trevor obtained his certificate of discharge from the Canadian Forces, signed by C.W. Peck, Captain, and John A. Hall, Lieut. Colonel, Commanding the 30th Battalion, CEF. Three days later he signed the Attestation Paper agreeing to serve in the Welsh Army. It was done.

The "Grand Patriotic Gathering" held in Pender Hall in Vancouver on January 20, 1915, was put on to "Celebrate the departure of Vancouver's contingent to Lloyd George's Welsh Army," so the foreword on the program said, and added, "This contribution to the Imperial Forces has been made possible by the patriotic generosity of Messrs. R. and C.M. Marpole." It was a program of addresses and stirring Welsh songs. The twenty guests of honour beamed with pleasure at all the fuss being made over them.

The Canadian Pacific's *Grampian* was two-funnel ship under the command of Captain J. Williams when she sailed from St. John to Liverpool on January 29th, 1915. The Welsh Contingent had comfortable staterooms which Mr. Marpole had thoughtfully booked so that they were adjacent to one another. The voyage was uneventful, and Trevor had an easy time carrying out his assignment. From Liverpool it was a short trip to Llandudno on the north coast of Wales and nearby Colwyn Bay, where he handed over his charges to Lieutenant-Colonel Wm. Hamar Greenwood, Commanding Officer of the 10th Service Battalion, South Wales Borderers of the Welsh Army Corps. Then he was off for the promised three weeks leave before reporting for duty.

Meta had not yet received his letter telling of this change in plans and naturally thought he was still in Canada. To have him at the door suddenly like this was unbelievable. It was an equally unexpected and happy reunion with the other members of his family, brothers, sisters, his parents, and the Taylors.

Nine years had passed since Morgan and Rachel Williams had seen this adventuresome son of theirs. Morgan's beard, beginning to grey when Trevor left, was now completely white. Both parents, erect and trim, were now in their early seventies. Morgan, fairly bursting with pride, took his uniformed son around to his favourite pub to show him off to his cronies. Rachel, like Meta, agonizingly fearful of her son's entry into this terrible war, managed to conceal her feelings to a degree, but hugged him tightly . . . as though by her willing it, he would come through safely and unharmed.

When he subsequently reported for duty, Trevor was officially enrolled with a Swansea regiment, the 14th Welsh, and on March 2nd was promoted to the rank of Lieutenant. Hart Jenkins, now Major Jenkins, had joined the 25th Northumberland Fusiliers, a crack regiment, and he urged Trevor to follow suit. After some months Trevor did apply for the transfer. It was a wise decision. On September 7, 1915, the move was approved, and with it came a promotion to the rank of Captain. He was now in the 25th Service Battalion, (2nd Tyneside Irish) Northumberland Fusiliers. "Fine bunch of chaps in this outfit," he wrote Meta. "It is especially good to be in with Hart . . ." He was posted to the Divisional Headquarters, Salisbury Plain, and granted leave to visit Swansea in mid-September.

November 1914. Many familiar faces were seen in uniform. All the men in this group are from the north end of Graham Island, with the exception of Colonel Cy Peck.

Left to right, top row: Richardson (of Graham Centre), Reg Partridge, cousin of Dodgson (next row), Ernie Wearmouth, next two unknown, then Smith, and last man unknown, from North Beach area.

Middle row: Dodgson (cabin was on Mexican Tom Trail), about two miles from Port Clements, Partridge lived with him), Bert Entwistle, Red Metcalfe, Bob Entwistle, Trevor Williams, Holyroyd (worked for the surveyors) and Bert Wearmouth.

Bottom row: D.M. McKay (who knelt to say his prayers despite his surroundings), Fred Batchelor, Jim Hammond (Nellie's husband), Col. Cy Peck, Alan Jessup and unknown man at end.

Photo–Charlie Ives

In January 1915, Trevor transferred to the Welsh contingent being sponsored by Messrs R. and C.M. Marpole and was put in charge of the twenty-one men sent overseas under this arrangement.

Arriving in North Wales a few weeks later, he was enrolled with a Swansea regiment, the 14th Welsh, and promoted to lieutenant. But in September Hart Jenkins urged him to join his 25th Service Battalion (2nd Tyneside Irish), Northumberland Fusiliers.

Shortly after, he was made a captain—and this photo taken.

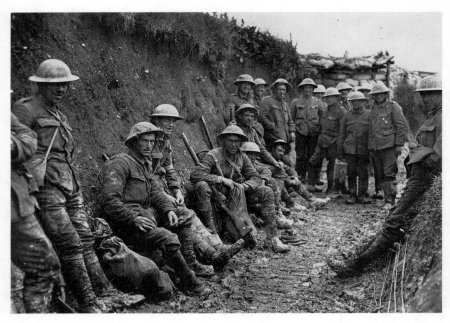
July 6, 1916. British soldiers in the trenches. Few would survive.
Photo courtesy Imperial War Museum, London, England

British troops near Thieval–1916. Mud, misery, death and desolation.
Photo courtesy Imperial War Museum, London, England.

FOURTEEN

IF THERE IS ONE ASPECT of history which remains unchanged throughout the ages, it is the total folly of war. Those who ill-advisedly initiate wars further compound their error in the strategists they put in charge. An error all too often repeated by those on whom they have declared war, when a high command will consist of men who are routine-bound, enmeshed in orthodoxies grown monstrous—out of touch with the realities of the battlefield of the day.

In the 1914–1918 war the gross mistakes of the generals on all sides resulted in the mechanical butchery of millions of men in the bloodiest conflict in history. Any victories on the muddy, crater-strewn fields were bought so dearly as to be nearly indistinguishable from defeat. Hundreds of thousands of men died in battles fought for an anonymous yard of inconspicuous mire and were sent again and again into futile massacre. "Soldiers so brave the heart falters at the thought of them," wrote one observer. And a historian commented, "A generation of men are being eliminated, not only in those killed, but also in the ruined lives of the blinded, wounded, and maimed and those whose minds have been shattered by the strain of unbelievable horror."

At the onset all sides believed the war would be over in months, and scenes of mobilization were often gay and carefree. Pluck and verve would win the day. And from the crowds of eager young men besieging the recruiting offices, only the cream of the crop were selected.

In Britain at the end of 1914 governmental communiques were full of optimism—an optimism greatly at odds with some of the news which seeped through from the front. True, the German advance did appear to have been halted. But their troops were still well within the borders of both Belgium and France, and a baffling deadlock had developed, with neither side able to force any gain despite repeated attempts. Casualties were already in the hundreds of thousands. French losses in the first five months were estimated to be over 360 thousand, Germans some two hundred thousand, and more than half the crack British professionals had been wiped out. This small force sent by Britain at the beginning of the war was probably man for man the best military group anywhere. Their rifle fire was so accurate and rapid the Germans believed they were machine-gunners. But they were inexpertly administered.

In some knowledgeable British circles, there were guarded mutterings about ill-planned strategy, of generals having greatly underestimated the strength of the German army. There were rumours of insufficient trench artillery when troops were sent into action—some field commanders reported that less than one fifth of needed supplies had been delivered. Communications, the life-line of any battle, were unorganized. The machine-guns which the Germans were using with such devastating effect were dismissed by the British High Command as "very much over-rated," and they would only issue two such guns per battalion.

Sir John French, commander-in-chief of the British Forces, managed to field criticisms, saying that improved plans were in hand and everything would go much better in 1915.

But by the end of 1915 the news was even worse. An Expeditionary Force sent to the Dardenelles in April of that year (a move which from the beginning had been cursed by informed strategists in western Europe for drawing much-needed men and supplies from what was considered a more urgent front) had been so mishandled that over 250 thousand men were lost in a series of fiascoes with nothing accomplished. The survivors, withdrawn near the end of 1915, had brought back tales of incredible misery. Sacrifices had been useless.

At the same time, more and more troops were being mobilized and poured into France. Terrible battles raged. Casualty lists were mind-boggling. Trainloads of wounded returning from the front told first-hand stories of men needlessly lost in offensives planned by commanders ignorant of the realities of the situation. The appalling truth of the war was becoming difficult to hide with cheerful propaganda about glorious victories and steady progress.

Prime Minister Herbert Asquith was forced to resign in May, 1915, and a coalition under David Lloyd George took over. Lloyd George's first move was to set up a Ministry of Munitions to specifically remedy the shortage of artillery. Then, as talk of mismanagement persisted, Sir John French was relieved of his command in December of that same year. He was replaced by General Sir Douglas Haig. But they had simply exchanged one commander for another equally out of touch with the nature of the war. Haig, unable to comprehend the facts of trench warfare, thought in terms of a great cavalry charge. Staff officers in the HQ offices, those who took part in command decisions, were identified by a specific insignia. In the British Army these men wore red tabs. In the front lines, as the rift between men in the lines and those who made the decisions developed, the words "red tab" became an expression of derision. Headquarters were always far to the rear of the battlegrounds, housed in chateaus which were luxurious in comparison with the filth of the trenches. Senior staff officers stayed away from active front lines for fear that the sight of horribly wounded men might affect their judgement in ordering brutal attacks. General Haig said he considered it his "duty" to avoid even visiting casualty stations.

In contrast to the staff officers, line officers received the highest respect from the ordinary soldier. They shared the dangers and misery of the trenches and led the attacks. These officers suffered proportionally higher casualties than any other group, including enlisted men.

The rift between the men in the trenches and those in high command was in evidence on all sides. The French complained that those who planned their strategy had no understanding of the conditions under which their orders would be carried out. After the disastrous battle of Verdun in 1917, when the French army was nearly wiped out, the survivors actually mutinied, saying "the war must end." Somehow the mutineers were brought under control and promised that their lives would not be wasted in fruitless blood-baths. In Italy the soldiers cried out bitterly, "Let us march on Rome!"—such was the resentment created by their inept and callous command after a million men had been slaughtered in a stupid attempt to gain some of the most difficult terrain in the war. The Germans also deplored the fact that their commanders seldom, if ever, came near their trenches, and although the Germans initially had the benefit of better preparation and equipment, their commanders were fatally indecisive at crucial times, a failing which needlessly cost thousands of lives.

The year of 1915 closed without any ray of victory. The hopelessness of those in the field was typified in a letter found on a dead German soldier. "This war is just a gigantic seige on both sides," he had written. "The whole front is one endless fortified trench from the coast of Belgium to the Swiss border. It is a war of attrition. Neither side can win. We can only go on hopelessly, millions of men massed together like moles in a network of underground mud." His letter would certainly never have passed his army's censors, but it found kindred understanding with an enemy who retrieved and translated it.

As 1916 dawned, all sides were told to be prepared for even bigger battles. The deadlock *must* be broken—no matter what the cost.

It was into this situation on January 1, 1916, that Trevor received his orders to go to France. The troops Britain sent into the field that year were considered highly trained and in peak condition. Trevor, as a captain in the 25th Northumberland Fusiliers, 103 Brigade, was in the advance party of the 34th Division. He bought a small notebook to use as a field diary, and the following pages are direct quotations from that book.

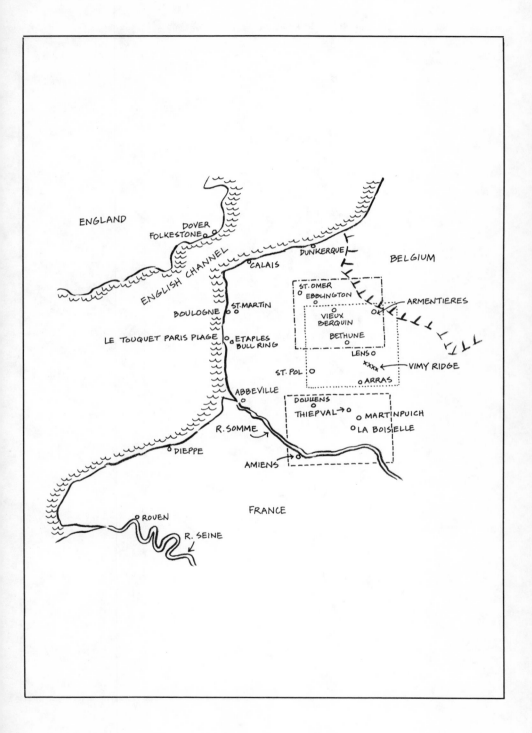

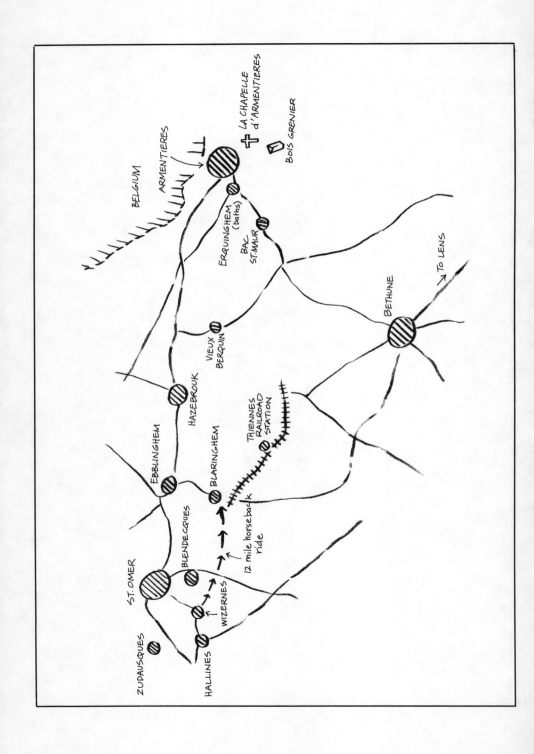

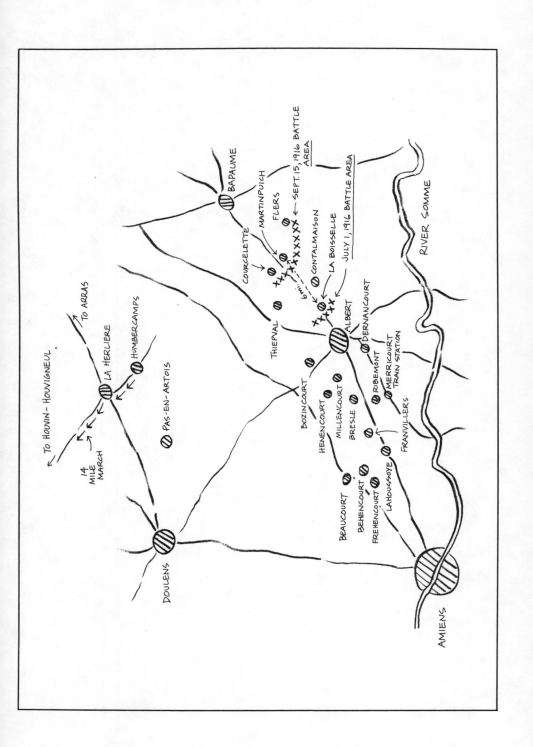

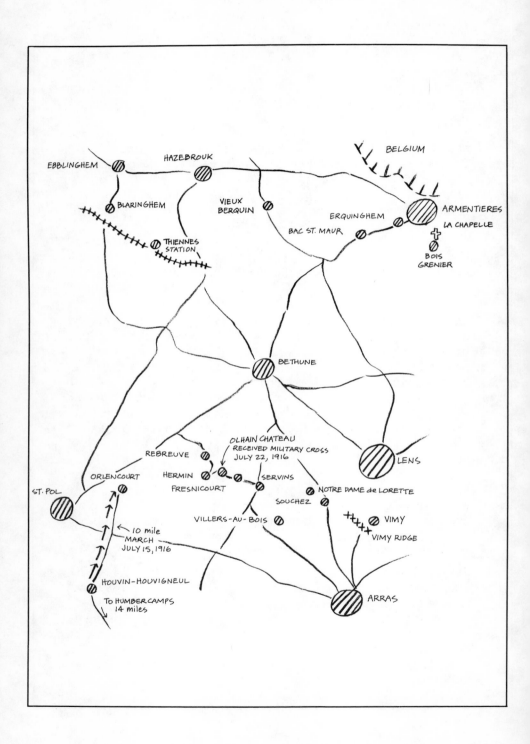

Jan 2:   Left Southampton at 7 a.m. Rough crossing to Le Havre where we arrived at 3 p.m. Boat jammed with troops and supplies. Two destroyers escorted us all the way. Most of the men seasick, so there was a fine mess. I kept off my feet and luckily kept my stomach down.

Our party consists of Lieut.Col. Wilkins, GSO 1, of the 34th HQ staff; Major Lawler, 15th Royal Scots; Captain Baker, Lincoln Regt.; Captains Gracie and McLay of the Tyneside Scottish; Captain Morkell, Royal Engineers; Lieut. Lomas, Royal Artillery and another officer for the Divisional Ammo Column; Captain Mackenzie, 24th Northumberland Fusiliers; and myself of the 25th Northumberland. Plus ten batmen.

In Le Havre reported to Base HQ and told to stand by. Put up at the Hotel Modom on Boulevard de Strasburg, and eight of our party went to see a French play in the evening. It is fourteen years since I lived in this town (when I worked for Monsieur Taconet in the brokerage firm). The place is now full of troops and very interesting.

Jan 3:   Lt. Col. Wilkins, chief of our party, called a meeting to give out orders. Captain Gracie (Tyneside Scottish), Baker (of the Lincolns), myself, and a Lieut. Jackson (Coldstream Guards) are to proceed to Boulogne tonight. Train was packed. Managed to sleep sitting up in our coats after a fashion. Stopped at Rouen at 4 a.m. and told there would be no train to Boulogne until evening. Jackson and I took a look around Rouen, particularly admiring the fine cathedral. There is a refreshment room in the railway yard run by some cheerful English girls, who keep the place open day and night for soldiers passing through. A service much appreciated.

Left Rouen at 9 p.m. Lots of room, so able to stretch out for a sleep until 2 a.m. when we were routed off at Abbeville for another long wait. Got away from Abbeville at noon and into Boulogne by 4 p.m. Reported to the DAQMG who knew nothing! Told to stand by until information received. Put into Hotel Metropole; nice place, good grub, but we want to get on with our regiments.

Jan 6:   There's been a mix-up. My battalion now not slated to arrive until 12th or 13th. Nothing to do but wait. Went to meet the Folkestone boat to see how troops are handled on landing. Met Major Reece, 15th Welsh, who brought over a draft, also Capt. Jeffries of 6th Welsh. This waiting around is boring, so offered to help Lieut. Marescaux in the MLO (Military Landing Office). He's a fine chap, and we get on well. All troops and ships have to report to this place and be assigned—its an interesting place to work.

Jan 8:   Went to the quay this afternoon to meet the first troops of our division, a half battalion of the 11th Suffolks, who have been sent to St. Martin's Camp on the outskirts of Boulogne.

Jan 9: Very pleasant working with Marescaux in the MLO. I have my meals with the other officers, many of whom are French— interesting to talk to. Met two more boats today. At 1 p.m. the other half of the 11th Suffolks arrived, then at 4:30 p.m. the 23rd Northumberland Fusiliers landed. The full battalion with pipes at their head, marched out to St. Martin's Camp. They had a great reception through Boulogne.

Jan 10: General Williams, GOC of the 34th Division arrived at noon on the mail-boat. Another mix-up as he was not expected, and he had to wait until he could leave in a car for the GHQ at St. Omer. Shortly before this the 26th Northumberland Fusiliers landed. They have been put into St. Matin's Camp for tonight, but will go on to St. Omer tomorrow. Captain Harold Price, whom I last saw on Graham Island where he was a surveyor, is with this outfit. (Price surveyed my preemption.) German mines were found this afternoon near Folkestone, so all cross-channel sailings stopped.

Jan 11: Mines were swept, and cross-channel traffic resumed this afternoon. The 27th Northumberland Fusiliers landed at 5:30. I met them and saw them off to camp. Learned there is a change of plans for the 25th NF (my battalion). They are to land at Calais, not here. So made arrangements to leave tomorrow. Gracie and Baker also going with me. Will stay in St. Omer area to meet our battalions.

Jan 14: Billeted in the cure's house with Harold Price of the 26th NF. The priest and his housekeeper, though much inconvenienced by having us in their small house, nevertheless are very polite and helpful. I take my meals with the 26th NF in a local cafe. We are in Wizernes, a little to the SW of St. Omer. Yesterday I walked over to Hallines to see Major Arden, Staff Captain for the 103rd (my) infantry brigade. He was sweating and swearing at having to find billets for the 25th NF and seemed relieved to have help. Gave me a map of the billeting area from here to Blendecques with a list of possible sites. A local guide and I spent a busy time yesterday visiting these places. Found my French useful.

Was roused out of bed at 7 a.m. to meet an advance party of the 25th NF who had arrived by train. Put this lot into billets, then borrowed a horse to ride to Blendecques where I found the rest of the 25th and showed them to their billets. I am acting as interpreter and billet officer for the whole battalion—a job which will keep me hopping.

Jan 15: Busy fixing up the billets with latrines and wash places. Moved my billet from the cure's to be nearer our mess. Route marches and rapid fire practices to begin tomorrow for the battalions.

Jan 17: Long route march again this morning. Passed a lot of fine French trenches and defence works which were a revelation. The French have a line right across this district—miles behind the lines—in case of retreat. Two Boche planes dropped bombs on the GHQ in St. Omer today in broad daylight. Anti-aircraft defence very feeble.

Jan 18: Granted a short leave today so went into St. Omer to see Clifford Taylor, Meta's younger brother, who is with the Artists Rifles, an Officers Training Corps unit. He is chafing at barrack and guard duty at the GHQ. Wants to get into action. Showed me round St. Omer including where the bombs had dropped yesterday.

Jan 19: More route marching this morning. Had the men bathe their feet. Very fine and mild. Gas helmet drill, bayonet fighting, and general battalion drill.

Jan 20: Ordered to march out five miles for a review by Sir Douglas Haig and General Joffre. The entire 34th Division was drawn up beside the road and had to stand and wait for them for two hours. Very cold and raining today. When the big chiefs arrived they went slowly along the line in a car. Soon over. Everyone disgusted at the long, cold wait for such a performance.

Jan 21: Rapid loading, bayonet fighting, and drill. Was put in full charge of the company all day as Captain Murray is away at a machine-gun course. Had a gas helmet inspection and found over a dozen fatally defective helmets. This discovery did not go down well with Murray, who took it as a personal criticism instead of a means of saving lives.

Jan 24: Moved from Wizernes to Blaringhem, twelve miles east. Two companies and all the HQ staff billeted on one farm. Very crowded. Orderlies pretty slack, and it was after 10 a.m. before we got breakfast. A general parade and inspection ordered for the visit of Lieut Gen. Poulteney, Army Corps Commander, this afternoon. He made a speech. Cleaned up and organized billets.

Feb 3: Still at Blaringhem. Daily route marches, drilling, bayonet fighting, plus practice in erecting wire entanglements. HQ sent me to both Ebblington and Thiennes Stations to report on road conditions and facilities for loading troops. Went on horseback for both trips—about eight or nine miles to Ebblington, return, and some ten or twelve miles to Thiennes and return. Wrote Meta tonight to remind her to pay our taxes on Lot 997, Graham Island. How far away it seems.

Feb 6:   We move towards the front line trenches near Armentieres tomorrow. I was sent to find billets for the whole battalion. Major Arden came with me as far as Vieux Berquin, our first stop. Have been doing night fighting practice this last while—this includes trench bombing and wire-cutting.

Feb 8:   We are now between the big guns and the front lines, and firing can be plainly heard. Some of the battalion are billeted at Bac St. Maur, about four miles west from Armentieres and the rest near Erquinghem, some two miles west. The guns behind us fired constantly this afternoon. We go into the trenches tomorrow night.

Feb 9:   Went up by platoons in the dark—I went with the 14th platoon and joined "B" company of the 10th Northumberlands. Will be attached to the 10th NF (in the line) for instruction. Spent the night with them at Charley's Farm, near Bois Grenier, a couple of miles south of Armentieres. These are reserve trenches about a half mile from the actual front line.

Feb 10:   Some of our men sent to occupy a strong point known as Cemetery Post near Bois Grenier. The post is the church graveyard with headstones utilized as parapets and shelters. Bois Grenier is in ruins, but the church spire is still standing and used as an observation post. I went up in it today to look over the trench area. No one visible during the day, however gramophones could be heard in some of the cellars. At night the place is very busy. Lots of traffic with ration and ammunition parties as well as trench reliefs. On the German side the same thing must be going on.

We went into the front line along 'Shaftesbury Avenue,' a heavily bagged and airy, roomy, communications trench. Passed through some heavy machine-gun firing . . . first bullets so close since South Africa. Everyone very nervous and strung up now that we are in the front line.

Feb 11:   A relatively quiet night, luckily—only one man hit. However, there was a big strafe during the day. Most of it seemed to go over our heads, but the sandbags were knocked around all over the place. Nothing to do but bear it—a trying ordeal, but the men stood it well. Raining all day and these trenches in terrible shape. Owing to the heavy shelling no repair work could be done. Lots of shrapnel. After dark we were sent to the reserve billets of the 13th DLI for the night. I am attached to their "B" Company.

Feb 12:   Billets shelled so heavily that we had to leave them twice and take the men into the funk holes (cellars and trenches prepared for such an emergency). The strafe seemed general, and the front line was also heavily shelled. Went back into the front line tonight with "B" Company of the DLI under Lieut. Long. Took over from the 12th DLI Trenches in bad shape after today's strafe. We were busy all night filling sandbags, repairing wire, and mending breaches. One man was shot alongside me on the parapet. These trenches are all built up with sandbags and revetments. The water is close under and every shell hole and depression full. Some job to find earth to fill sandbags. Should one step off the duckboards one becomes immediately mired to the waist—a treacherous situation in the dark.

Feb 13:   Morning quiet, but all hell broke loose in the afternoon. Continuous shelling with HE (heavy artillery) and shrapnel for hours. Seemed impossible that anyone could survive. I surely expected every moment to be my last. Miraculously only four men killed and five wounded. There is nothing to be done but just suffer under these barrages, and it is the greatest strain. One's inclination is to get into one of the sandbag shelters, which is dangerous as under a direct hit they would collapse and bury one alive. Though they are proof against fragments. Had the greatest of admiration for Lieut. Long moving about during the shelling. Forced myself to accompany him, but found it difficult to keep my attention from the bursting shells. A tough experience for our first day. Left the front lines after dark and went into the reserve billets. Complicating my problems is a bad case of dysentery. Did see the MO about it. He gave me some pills and told me to rest! Some advice for a PBI (Poor Bloody Infantryman).

Feb 15:   After one night in the reserve trenches we were sent last night to Rue Marle, near Armentieres, to relieve the 1st Worcester. I had to take two platoons up in support of the frontlines and stand-to alert all night. Sleet, rain, and very cold. No sleep possible for anyone. So today spent most of time in bed in reserve trench. Feeling rotten with this damned diarrhoea. Reserve area shelled all day. Casualties. Strong wind and heavy rain.

Feb 17:   Took a working party up to the frontlines and repaired the salient at 124, near the estaminet (coffee shop) at Rue Marle. Were ready to return when the Boche started shelling the entrance of our company trench. Had to wait it out until they finished.

Feb 18:   About a hundred big 5.7 shells were dropped near us this morning. We took over some reserve trenches on 'Cowgate Avenue' from "A" Company, 20th NF. Main dugouts in these support trenches are not bad but the officers shelters are grim.

Feb 19:   Very exposed and under fire by day and night. Trying to shave this morning when a big shell burst outside the dugout—so suspended that operation. Went into battalion HQ this afternoon and told Wally Jones, the acting CO, that we had been seven days without any blankets in this cold weather. He told me we are to be relieved tomorrow.

Feb 20:   Two of our planes over the lines near us were strongly shelled by the Boche. The shrapnel and fragments fell in our lines. At night my company told to leave the lines. Took over billets from "C" Company at La Chapelle d'Armentieres. This place has been badly shelled and no windows left anywhere, so it is draughty and cold. So near the front lines we are constantly shelled.

Feb 21:   Went into Armentieres. Had tea in a nice cafe—an extraordinary find within range and sound of evening guns. Lots of women, children, and civilians in the town despite the shells coming over every day. Our big guns in and round La Chapelle d'Armentieres fire steadily. Reports are deafening.

Feb 23:   Left billets in La Chapelle d'Armentieres last night and came into the trenches near the estaminet, relieving the "D" Company 26th NF. Very dark after the snow and sleet during the day. The trenches were sopping. Up all night posting the men. It was freezing cold all day today. Fairly quiet until noon when our guns did some shelling of the front, and the Boche retaliated on us. More snow and frost tonight—everyone suffering with the cold. On watch from midnight to 4 a.m. Freezing hard again. Strafe on our left and gas alarm on our right. Everyone nervous.

Feb 25:   Snowing and freezing. Very dark at night. Posted double sentries in each bay until 4 a.m. when I put on single men.

Feb 27:   Court of Inquiry at 9:30 a.m. in the trenches yesterday. Self-inflicted wound of Private Hunt. I was President and ruled that it was an accident. The men are so miserable there is a good chance they will deliberately wound themselves to get into hospital. Relieved last night by the 26th NF and marched out to rest billets near the baths at Erquinghem. Just as everyone got to sleep, worn out with fatigue and exposure, we had a gas alarm and all had to turn out and stand-to. Some job to wake them and get them out in the dark. False alarm and we all turned in again about midnight. Back to bed and slept until noon. It is a great relief to be out of the fire—although we could see shells being dropped on Armentieres.

Feb 29:   Went to the orderly room at HQ this morning as Capt. Murray had made a complaint that I was of no help to him. I was disgusted as he's never said a word to me. He is drinking far too much and I suspect this is a cover-up—plus he may still harbour resentment about my discovery of those defective gas helmets in his charge on Jan 21st. He is not a good officer. Made a request to be transferred to another company. It is enough to fight this damned war without putting up with this sort of nonsense.

Mar 4:   Snowing heavily and thawing by turns. Slush everywhere. Trenches are flooded and miserable. Wiring parties have been out each night putting up new wire, and there have been several big strafes from our side. No one gets much sleep. Relieved tonight by the 23rd Tyneside Scottish who were late, so it was 10 p.m. before we left the front lines. Then had to march six miles to our billets, caked with mud, wet and weary. Halted for tea about 11 p.m. and finally got to our billets at 3 a.m. Everyone tired out. Quite a job to keep the men together.

Mar 7:   Went with working party to La Vessee post and spent most of p.m. repairing trenches, then marched home—fourteen miles in the mud all told. Snow and thaw all day. Tomorrow will take the men to the baths in Erquinghem. These baths are a fine institution; there will be a complete change of clothes for every man after his bath.

Mar 10:   Inspected company and tried to make the men clean themselves for an inspection by the CO, Lieut. Col. Beresford. I was told I will be staying with this company for the present—a transfer not advised. I was OC for today as Capt. Murray at a Court Martial on Lieut. Maguire, whom he had accused of being drunk. Maguire was honourably acquitted.

Mar 15:   Marched to brigade reserve billets near Canteen Farm yesterday to relieve the 15th Royal Scots. The Germans had four observation balloons in sight, and as it was a fine day with the relief going on, we expected to catch it. Heavy shelling on the roads, but only six shells came near us. Fine clear night. The Germans sent up clouds of smoke to our right, and we gave them rapid fire. Then they swept our line with machine-gun fire and sent over some shrapnel.

Mar 17:   Late last night I was told to take a fatigue party of seventy-eight men to carry RE stores up to the front line. Only twelve men were actually required for this, and all the rest had to wait under continuous rifle fire and machine-gun attack. I reported these facts to HQ on my return.

Out of the lines today and all the men trying to get drunk on French beer without much success.

Mar 22: Quite a bit of activity in the trenches. Machine-guns and shrapnel sweeping our lines, and we return with rapid fire. Went out with wiring party last night in front of our lines. This business of exposing oneself in No Man's Land, even at dark, is a nervous affair. Rifle fire is going on all the time regularly. Sentries fire at marks taken by day or at the flacks in the opposite trenches. Bursts of machine-gun fire occur—the Boche being very good at spraying the top of our parapet. Verey lights go up frequently, and an occasional shell goes over or lands nearby. There is a lot of ducking into shell holes or stretching out flat in the mud.

On watch from 4 a.m. after wiring completed. Enemy parapet visible at 5:15 a.m. today.

Guns going strong all day on both sides. Enemy shells set fire to four buildings about three hundred yards from our reserve billets—some of our guns were there. Also blew up the ammunition dump. The artillery people lost everything in their billets, which were also blown up and burned.

Apr 1: Went to brigade bombing school for a bombing course. Lieut. Pantin is OC in charge of this course, and there is a large store of bombs and hand grenades. Pantin keeps bombs of all kinds in his hut, and as they are live ones, his casual way of handling them is alarming. I helped him unload some bombs and rifle grenades this evening, and although there was no explosion, I certainly fully expected one.

Apr 3: Still at the bombing school. German planes over us and much anti-aircraft firing. Very fine and warm—seems a shame to have a war going on in such glorious weather. My battalion went into the trenches this evening, but I was told to stay at the bomb course. Moved my valise to Pantin's hut and slept with him and his explosives. Our CO Lieut. Col Beresford, went on leave today, and we hear he will not return. Wally Jones now acting CO with Hart Jenkins second in command.

Apr 7: Back in the trenches for several days now. Three Germans came through the company on right. Deserters or lost. One was captured and two escaped behind our lines. Had search parties out looking for them. No luck.

The ruins of the Albert Cathedral with the large statue hanging down. It was said that as long as the statue did not fall, neither would the city of Albert.
Photo courtesy Imperial War Museum, London, England

British troops in support trench prior to attack on Beaumont Hamel, north
of Thieval. Soldiers trying to get some rest despite the narrow, cramped
conditions.
Photo courtesy Imperial War Museum, London, England

Apr 8: Quiet day in the billets. Visited by several Australians. Their division recently arrived in France from Gallipoli and are going to take over our lines in this district. Some NCO's of the 19th Australian Battalion, 5th Brigade, came round this afternoon to take over our billets (as we are soon to move to another area). Fine, clean-looking men, but over-confident. After Gallipoli they feel they have nothing to learn. One of their battalions is already in the line relieving a Scottish battalion. First day in the trenches some of them stood on the parapet and waved their big hats and shouted to the Germans. Five of them were instantly killed.

Later, to our horror and surprise we saw a large body of Australians in their big hats—they disdain steel helmets—marching towards the trenches in columns of fours in broad daylight. As the German observation balloon was up, we expected them and everyone else in the vicinity to be bombarded. Probably the Germans were too stunned at the sight to react for awhile. That body did escape, but the Aussies had barely reached the trenches when the Boche put down a barrage which caught and killed several of our gunners.

Apr 15: We have been moved to Zudausques, a village some five to six miles west of St. Omer, with the battalion billeted in the town hall of this small place, or nearby. I found a room in a farmhouse near our company mess and struck pure gold. The dear old French lady put me in a fine bed and even put hot bricks in for my feet. Some billet! Had a wonderful sleep. Captain Arden, DSO, is to take command of the 25th NF. This is excellent news as Arden, who has been acting as Staff Captain of the 103rd (our) Brigade, is a fine chap. He has been a New Zealand sheep farmer and is a first-rate soldier, with no frills.

Plenty of company drill as usual. Following this today, I visited the farms to arrange laundry for the men. I am the acting billeting officer and came in advance of the men to set up all arrangements, before we moved here. The padre had dinner with us tonight. We only see this bird when we are miles behind the lines, although he is supposed to be with us—attached for rations and duty. Heavy showers today. Practiced night raiding. The GOC is very keen on these raids on the German trenches, but no one else is.

May 2: Another long field day, practicing trench assault. Up at 4 a.m. and on the site by 8 a.m. until late in the afternoon, before the five-mile hike back to quarters again. Hard lines on the farmers to spoil their cultivated fields. There was a conference for Company Commanders afterwards with General Plumer which lasted for two hours. I remember him from South Africa (Plummer's Horses). He talked like a platitudinous old dug-out today. We have orders to move and packed tonight for a start tomorrow morning.

May 13: We are billeted in Albert now. Arrived here after a succession of stops. Hart Jenkins has just returned from leave and gave me news of Meta. With all our moves lately the mail has not been coming through too well. I am due for leave in a day or two.

Albert is much damaged by shells but plenty of good houses. No civilians. The fine big church with the huge image hanging down from the top of the spire causes much comment. And many superstitions —the commonest is that as long as the figure hangs there without falling, Albert also will not fall. Some big guns were being set up next to our billet when we came, and as those gunners also wanted our place, we were glad to vacate. Those guns are bad neighbours, drawing shell-fire and making a fearful noise. Each night we send work parties to the front line, and as the front lines are only thirty feet apart in places, these parties are dangerous affairs.

May 17: My leave warrant arrived at 6 p.m. last night. Got permission from the CO to leave the trenches—want no stray bullet spoiling my first leave. Camped in the QM stores for the night and was awakened at 2 a.m. by a runner from HQ with my ticket. Joy! Found that Bainbridge's leave ticket was enclosed with mine in error. Went round to the 26th NF and sent one of their runners up the line with Bainbridge's ticket. Waited for him until 8:30 a.m., then took a horse and rode to Merricourt to catch the train for Le Havre, where I arrived at 11 p.m. and boarded the *Monas Queen* for Southampton. No beds or blankets, but who cares. Travelled all night sleeping on a bench.

May 18: Arrived Southampton at 9:30 a.m. and immediately telegraphed Meta. Then to London and booked in at the Hotel Cecil. Meta was on the train from Swansea which got into Paddington Station at 9:30 that night.

May 21: London streets are full of well-dressed people, and life seems very gay after France. We took in several shows—Bing Boys at Alhambra, Joyland Review at the Hippodrome, and then Bric-a'brac at the Palace. The theatres are crowded and seats hard to get. Went to West Hamstead and called on brother Gwilym and his wife, Evelyn. It took us an hour to find their flat. Called at the Army and Navy stores about the battalion drums, then round London all day. Had some extravagant meals and gradually began to relax again. Caught the train to Swansea today. Father, Mother, and Jack Taylor met us at the Swansea station. It has been arranged for us to stay a few days at

Strathmore with the Taylors in Mumbles, then finish up at Troed-y-bryn with my parents.

May 25: The weather has been good for my entire leave. Walked the cliffs and loafed on the beaches at Caswell and Langland Bay and had a fine picnic near Three-Cliffs Bay. Little Jackie is growing like a weed. Visited Jack and Gwen Taylor, and saw the new baby. Meta's sister, Freda, also staying at Strathmore with her little girl, Gwyneth—about Jackie's age. There was a big do at the Royal Hotel in Swansea for Father, to which we went. Some of his friends put on an evening and presented him with a cigar case for his birthday. It was hard to say goodbye.

Came back to London this morning, thence to Southampton where I again sailed on the old packet *Monas Queen* for the trip to Le Havre.

May 28: My battalion out of the trenches and billeted at Bresle, a few miles west of Albert on the highway to Amiens. Fine weather fortunately as we are very crowded. Officers are in tents and men in billets. We are spending long field days practicing trench assaults and ruined a lot of fine growing crops with our manoeuvres—sorry for the hard-working French men and women who are not given any consideration by the HQ staff. Sunday today. Church parades which are not compulsory. This means a loaf for the majority who are not strong for the padres. Worked for three hours this afternoon bayonet fighting, throwing bombs, and trench digging.

June 2: Told to act as Quartermaster for the battalion while the QM Lieut. Cooper goes on leave. Cooper showed me the ropes today. The battalion to be split up tomorrow, five hundred to go to Albert, fifty-six to Dernancourt, and the rest to Behencourt. As acting QM I only have to look after the Behencourt party, the others being attached for rations to other units. Went to the ASC dump at Ribemount and borrowed a wagon for the six-mile move to Behencourt. Sent wagon-loads of baggage there in the morning then saw that the rest was loaded and away in the evening. Rode to Behencourt to meet the battalion on its arrival at 10 p.m.

June 6: Our supply dump is now at Frechencourt, about ¼ mile away. As I drew rations for nine hundred men yesterday and we only have three hundred men here, did not draw anything today and had little to do. Went over to see Harold Price (the ex-surveyor from Graham Island) of the 26th NF and had lunch with him. Later went for a walk with Alfred Depitres, the French interpreter and admired the beautiful country in this Somme Valley. This QM job is an easy one when the QMS and his help know their work as these men do.

June 7:   Went to Brigade HQ in Franvillers this afternoon to see about surplus stores due to change of billeting—we had been told to expect five hundred more, then they were sent elsewhere. Also saw Harold Price who had made a successful raid on the German trenches on the night of June 5th.

June 10:   Rain and thunder. Went for supplies as usual at Frechencourt and found that only bully and biscuit would be issued for the next two days. This hardship was inflicted on the men by a direct order of the Divisional OC General Williams, who stopped the fresh meat and bread. We get bully and biscuit as part of our rations and cannot understand why the fresh rations should be stopped.

June 12:   Lieut. Cooper returned from his leave tonight, but says he is not staying long as the CO has recommended his transfer home. This was news to me. Lots of troops going through here these days and continuous traffic at night. We are evidently getting ready for a pretty big push.

June 14:   Have been warned to be ready to move tomorrow. Practiced fire orders and signals with the CO in the field. Troops are moving towards the line all day and night.

June 15:   Alfred Depitres and I rode to Lahoussoye, south of here, and arranged for billets for the battalion. An RFC flying school is stationed here with monoplanes, also hundreds of big lorries as the MT men take up ammunition.

June 17:   Went with a working party in the London buses to Albert, then to the trenches to carry up trench mortar bombs. My party had to take up big bombs weighing two hundred pounds each. It was all a hundred men could do to take up fifteen of these bombs. Working parties go by bus to the trench area in the mornings and evenings—three hundred to four hundred men in each party. Guides meet them in Albert and take them off for all sorts of jobs: making new trenches and dugouts in the chalk, carrying water, bully and biscuits, bombs and trench mortar shells to dugouts and front lines, and so on. It is hard work but a darn sight better than occupying the trenches as the men get a bus ride each way and have comfortable billets to return to.

June 19:   Went with working party to Albert with the buses. Worked all night carrying ammunition, water, and Stokes gun shells from wagons which came up to the reserve trenches. These horse and wagon and lorry drivers are always in a hurry to get away from the trench area—though at this point they are about a mile from the front line by way of communication trenches or over the top when the going is good enough and evening fire quiet. We finished about 3 a.m. and took the buses back to Lahoussoye. Ten new officers reported for duty today. This brings us overstrength and ready for casualties. Percy Tickler, a member of the firm making the famous Tickler's Jam, known all over the army, is the OC of "B" Company, 25th NF. He went to Albert to study the ground over which we are to advance and brought back a report.

June 22: Harold Price has just been awarded the Military Cross—one of the first ones—for his successful raid on June 5th. Everybody very pleased with him as his raid brought back useful information. Before this stunt Price was not too popular. His Canadian manners and lack of ceremony causing problems with this very English battalion. Rode over to congratulate him and had lunch with him in Franvillers.

June 23: To Brigade HQ on a bicycle with my trench map and had it marked with new emergency road and trenches which have recently been made for the coming push. Then went in a bus to Albert and went over the emergency road we will use. Heavy rain and thunderstorms on way back in bus. One of our balloons broke away in the storm, and we saw it drifting over the German lines.

June 24: To Brigade HQ at Franvillers with all company officers and NCO's and studied the relief map of the German trenches and country beyond La Boisselle over which we are due to go. Also studied the aeroplane photographs of this district. Very interesting. In the afternoon there was a practice of rapid loading against a bank at the side of the road.

June 25: The preliminary bombardment for the push started tonight. All the big guns and howitzers and most of the artillery on a front of twenty miles. Much practicing of advancing in extended order in waves 150 yards apart.

June 26: Field day with the whole brigade. Ground marked out with flags to represent enemy trenches. Practiced our advance by timing columns of platoons. Warm and showery. Guns firing continuously day and night.

Later . . . Have just heard that Harold Price was killed last night on his second trench raid.

June 27: Fixed up a Tommy's uniform to wear in the advance when officers must dress like the men. Left our billets at Lahoussoye at midnight and marched towards Albert, round which we detoured. Stopped at 4 a.m. about daylight and bivouacked in the open. Find we have only been given three tarpaulins for the whole battalion.

June 28:   The transports brought up our valises and kitchens so at least got some food and tried to get some sleep, although it was very miserable without shelter as it rained heavily all day. We were alongside big guns which were pumping away day and night. It is rotten staff work to put the men to this hardship just before an attack. We might just as well have stayed in our billets instead of out in the rain all day and night.

June 29:   Marched back to Franvillers by platoons and were billeted in the village all day. Got a decent night's sleep after the exposure of yesterday. Everyone cursing the staff for this ridiculous bungling. We had been sent up forty-eight hours too soon.

June 30:   Moved out again last night to our former bivouac near Albert, arriving around 2 a.m. Spent day resting and planning our advance tomorrow. Everyone takes two days grub and water on his person. Steady bombardment going on. Received our attack orders. Dressed in a Tommy's uniform and had a large yellow patch sewn on my back. This is for planes to be able to recognize units in the advance. Each advance unit has a different marking.

My packsack contains a waterproof trench cape, sweater, pair of socks, candle and empty milk can (to boil water), waterbottle, small tins tea, sugar, biscuit, bully beef, and canned salmon, as well as a map case, field notebook, spare revolver, and ammunition. Also have a rifle, bayonet, revolver, and compass. Will wear knee-high trench boots, loose breeches, and tunic, plus steel helmet and gas mask. I have been detailed to act as the right battalion guide—to precede the leading platoon on the right of the battalion, which will take its course by me so as not to overlap the units advancing on both sides of us. Am only too aware of the responsible and very dangerous job ahead.

July 1:   Went into the trenches last night after dark in readiness for today's attack. Col. Arden, our CO, reviewed us in the dusk as we left our bivouac. He gave out a double issue of rum and greatly encouraged everyone by his cheerful bearing and confidence. As we passed him it was 'thumbs up, boys' to everyone. A fine man and leader. There was the greatest confusion in and round the trench area where thousands of men were advancing to their jumping-off places in the dark. We finally got to our place in the support trench just before dawn and had a terrifying, nerve-wracking ordeal waiting for zero hour—7:30 a.m. A waiting period in which it was better not to think.

From dawn until zero hour the concentrated artillery fire and trench mortar bombing with the two hundred-pound bombs was frightening and deafening. The air was filled with the shriek and hiss of our shells and the whole world seemed to vibrate. Some German shells fell near us, big ones, which we knew of by seeing and feeling the dirt from their explosions. We could not hear them in the din. Near and far the blackness was torn by guns firing in stabs of flame and we could hear the slamming as of iron doors by howitzers discharging in a great livid blaze and heavy double detonations. The noise was indescribable.

When there was light enough I picked out some landmarks and took a compass bearing for our course to and through the German trenches as far as I could see.

Zero hour was signalled not only by our watches but by the huge explosions of two big mines which had been laid under the enemy trenches at La Boisselle. These immense explosions rocked the earth where I lay. It seemed impossible that anyone could survive in their neighbourhood—if indeed any had lived through this awful bombardment. The dust raised by the mines obscured the light, and we moved off into this obscurity. Luckily I had the compass bearings.

From our jumping-off trenches to our front line, advancing in extended order, I was frantically waving and signalling to keep the leading line in place. We had to make our way through shell holes, old trenches, and barbed-wire entanglements, which HQ told us had been cut. Not so—damn them! Half-way through these obstacles enemy machine-guns started even before the dust had settled down.

It was unbelievable! Later we learned that the enemy emplacements were **in front** of their trenches, with loopholes, level with the ground, built of concrete. The HQ staff did not advise us of any of this. These emplacements were mostly uninjured by the shelling and went into action when our barrage was lifted.

I felt a light blow on my back when jumping a trench but did not know until that night that I had three machine-gun holes in my pack—on both sides. When we reached our front lines, vacated by the battalion in advance of us, we passed through a heavy counter-barrage of 5.7's. This front line was too wide to jump and had been bridged.

But there were not enough bridges. Only one in sight in my vicinity. The men had to converge to this bridge, which meant more casualties before they could spread out again. Very few men got over this trench, but looking back, I could see the next line coming down over the top of the ridge behind and starting down the slope we had crossed. I kept on across No Man's Land with about ten or twelve men scattered behind me. When within some sixty yards of the enemy trenches I looked back and found myself the only one in sight—and all alone. The machine-gun fire was continuous, so I lay down. At first I thought the advance had been stopped and the order had not reached me.

Started to crawl back, but several bullets hitting the ground near me soon induced absolute quiet. Looking back I saw the other lines of our men advance over the skyline and gradually disappear into the ground. Our advance formation was in lines of platoons in extended order—two platoons of "B" and "D" Companies in the front line ("B" Company on the right and behind me). Then other platoons of these companies interspersed with Lewis gunners and bombers. Then "A" and "C" Companies ("C" in support of "B") then HQ signallers, MO and stretcher bearers. That is nine lines or waves for each battalion. Two battalions had gone in front of us in the same formation, and we were to pass through these two battalions at designated points and stop and consolidate at a point about two miles from our starting place.

There was no sign of the two Scottish battalions which had preceded us except a number of men—or bodies—in or near the German fire. They could not have taken the German trenches as the firing of the machine-guns never stopped, and presently German riflemen appeared firing over their parapet.

It was hard to believe that these two full battalions were out of action, but I was forced to realize that such was the case. That our advance was stopped. And that I was to witness the slaughter of my own battalion which kept coming over the top of the ridge on the skyline—a perfect target—in waves at intervals of 150 yards until the last wave had appeared and gradually or quickly faded into the ground. The steadiness of the advance as ordered, in view of what they could see would happen to them, was magnificent. But what criminal folly to allow it!

I later learned that the brigadier and three battalion CO's had been killed, along with my CO, plus (Major) Hart Jenkins and the adjutant, the four company CO's, the RSM and four company SM's. All officers except myself and one lieutenant were out of action.

About sixty of our battalion had advanced beyond our front trench. The rest were stopped long before reaching this trench. Of these sixty men, some were casualties. They all lay out in the open, some distance behind me and were in constant danger. The German barrage on our trench kept up all day, and the German riflemen and machine-guns kept up a steady fire on these men in No Man's Land. Several made a rush back to the shelter of our trench, but few made it, and every body which moved was a target. I found this out instantly when I tried it and lay motionless nearly all day.

The grass and weeds into which I dropped were long enough to cover me from view when stretched flat. But I drew fire several times after taking a peep. There were two Germans leaning over their parapet about seventy yards from me taking pot shots at our wounded and sometimes me. They were not successful. The greatest risk was from the machine-guns which raked the ground in all directions. I had dirt thrown over me and one perforation through the slack of my breeches above the knee. Added to these troubles, after some delay, evidently word went back to our howitzers that these trenches in front were still occupied, and the howitzers began sending over six-inch shells. They made beautiful shooting on the section of the trench in front of me, causing the riflemen to disappear, but never fazing the machine-guns. Of course I was anticipating a 'short' to land on or near me through all this performance, but did not dare move on account of the machine-guns.

A 'short' from the German barrage might have been equally fatal, and some of these German shells did drop fearfully close. The sun was blazing and I perspired from several causes. Never did a hot summer day drag along so slowly and fearfully. Thoughts of a German counter-attack occurred to me. There seemed to be nothing to stop them. Except for the howitzers, not a single shot had been fired from our lines all day in this sector, which appeared completely abandoned.

With no hope of living through the day, angry at my position and bitter about my battalion, I had my revolver, rifle, and bayonet ready for any counter-attack, raid or reconnaissance and would have been happy to have taken a few Boche along with me. Their shooting of our wounded was a shocking thing to witness.

In the late afternoon and evening firing slackened, so about 9 p.m. I started a careful crawl backwards. Got about halfway before being spotted, and an MG opened fire on me. I curled up in a shallow shell hole which held most of me, but had to leave my feet over the edges. Got a slice shot off the heel of my left boot. After 10 p.m. started back again, found a gap in our wire and made a rush, leaping down into our front trench in the dark. Was very nearly bayonetted by some of our men crouching where I jumped and surprised everyone at my descent.

After fifteen hours exposure it was an infinite relief to get into that deep trench. I found a sergeant and corporal and about fifty men uninjured in the trench with scores uncounted of dead and wounded. Blood and bodies everywhere, only one dugout, crammed with dead and wounded. I blocked off a section on each side of the communication trench, organized a garrison from the survivors, posted sentries, and sent a report back to the brigade asking for orders—and spent a terrible night.

Wounded from the Scottish and our battalion kept coming in all night (which was very dark) until the trench became crowded and almost impassable. We were shelled heavily, causing more casualties and confusion. Sent another runner back to find brigade HQ with a report and asking for stretchers and permission to withdraw for reorganization.

July 2:   Towards dawn a Lieut. Col. and party (9th Welsh) from the 19th Division appeared and said he was going to stage a raid with two battalions of his division. He had been told this trench was unoccupied and had no orders regarding my detail. As it was impossible for these men to get into our crowded trench, and dawn was making them visible on top, I withdrew my party along the communications trench to the reserve trenches. Here we found plenty of RAMC (medical corps) men unoccupied—waiting for cases to be brought to them.

I sent them, much against their wish, to bring out our casualties and kept them at it until the trench was cleared of wounded. Then I went myself to Brigade HQ at Tara Redoubt where Lieut. Col. Stewart, OC of the 27th NF, was acting as brigadier. My appearance was a surprise. Neither of my reports had reached them. I had been reported as a casualty—missing. They had no news of the survivors of my battalion. I was the OC of the battalion—such as was left—and was ordered back to Belleview Farm with my unit.

Shortly after, another surviving officer, a 2nd Lieut., turned up and he took the men back. When I left the brigade HQ I was all in after two such days and nights without sleep. Put my pack down beside the main road and laid my head on it. Never heard the traffic or shelling for a couple of hours. Then went on to Belleview Farm, where we rested, refitted, and made all ready for another advance. Got a letter off to Meta.

July 3:   At Belleview Farm. This is a howitzer battalion and prisoner receiving station. The Provost Marshal in charge was very hospitable, and we soon recovered from our late experience. Stragglers kept coming in from the front where they had managed to survive in trenches and shell holes with other units. We also got some of the men and officers left with the transport before the push. Made our battalion strength up to 250 with all ranks. A few German prisoners came in—seemed glad to be taken, as the advance on our right had been successful, having taken and held the first two German trenches at La Boisselle where the mines killed the occupants.

From lodgings thus made, our holdings were gradually extended by bombing and shelling along the trenches. We were told to stand-by in reserve all day—ready to go in again if necessary. A new CO, Major Rose of the 15th Royal Scots, arrived this afternoon to take temporary command of the battalion.

July 4: Moved from Belleview Farm to a site between Bouzincourt and Millencourt, slightly southwest of Albert. Had to pitch tents for the whole division who came out of the trenches this morning. Heavy rain, mud, and misery. Camp is close to the trenches where the bombardment is continuous.

July 7: Day before yesterday moved camp from Bouzincourt to Henencourt Wood—then another, wet, muddy, miserable situation. Yesterday a.m. there was a parade of brigade survivors before Gen. Poulteney, 3rd Corps CO, who complimented the brigade on its behavior in the attack on July 1st. Major Rose left today to take command of his old regiment, and we were very sorry to see him go—a fine chap, very charming, hear he is from a wealthy Edinburgh family. In his place Major Temple, late 2nd in command of the 26th NF and who had stayed behind with the transport during the push, was put in command of our battalion.

Last evening another move. Big London buses took us from Henencourt Wood, through Albert and Amiens, then north to Doullens, from whence we drove along the road to Arras, turning off at Herliere, about halfway along, and then in to Humbercamps, arriving at 8 a.m., stiff and weary after being crowded inside and on top of the buses all night. At that time I was acting 2nd in command of the battalion and was put into a hut with Major Temple when I arrived. Find him a superior sort of a duck, but friendly enough—so far.

July 12: Much reorganization of men and companies as survivors are put together with those of other units. 25th and 26th NF forming one unit, whilst 24th and 27th form another. I am with the first bunch and OC of No. 2 Company. Temple is the Battalion OC and Bridges took over from me as 2nd in command. We now belong to the 37th Division, 7th Army Corps, 3rd Army. The HQ for the division is at Pas-en-Artois in a fine chateau.

At 10 a.m. our new divisional general, Count voie Gluchese, smothered in ribbons and accompanied by a fine shiny, bunch of brass hats, had a general inspection of the brigade. Battalion paraded en masse and the transport behind. Inspection went off alright.

Letter from Meta saying I had been reported missing. She had been telephoning all and sundry for news with little success. Got onto Gwilym who pestered the War Office until he found out I was not a casualty. My letter posted on the 3rd had still not reached her, and she had no word from 1st July to 11th—except the report that I was a casualty. The push had upset the postal service just when it was most necessary to reassure the folks at home. Wrote her again, also Gwilym. Had a letter from Marjorie Jenkins asking for particulars about her brother Hart's death. Company drill held in the afternoon with a lecture from Temple—which was not appreciated by anyone.

July 15:   Another move. Left Humbercamps last night and marched fourteen miles to Houvin-Houvigneul where we were billeted at 2 a.m. Hoped to have a decent sleep but were called at 7 a.m. and told to be ready to move at 9 a.m. Another march—ten miles this time—to Orlencourt where we billeted. Obviously we are on our way to Vimy Ridge. It was a hot and very fatiguing day for the men with their full packs after the long march last night. Though I had a horse to ride, I used the beast for giving lifts to the most weary and for carrying packs. Also took a pack myself to help the most footsore from time to time. The weight of these packs made me suspicious, and we had an inspection of same. Found that some of the packs contained souvenirs of the push—nose caps, shell fragments, and other heavy articles. Warned the men that they could pack anything they wished so long as they stayed in the ranks, but they would get no more help or free rides for their souvenirs when there were others who needed the help more legitimately. Any man who fell out on the march was deprived of his souvenirs and limited to his regulation pack—which is plenty heavy enough.

July 16:   Resting in billets at Orlencourt, a few miles roughly east of St. Pol. Had foot inspection and got the men to care for their feet. Note from Meta to say she had at last heard from me personally, but that there had been no news from the end of June until the 12th of July, except for the terse report that I was missing in action. Thank heavens for Gwilym's efforts with the War Office. Meta sent me a tobacco pouch for my birthday. I'll be thirty-six in two days.

July 17:   A great stack of letters arrived, including several from parents of sons lost on July 1st. Had to reassure them as best I could with particulars of the casualties—a miserable job. Death seems sufficiently final, but some parents wanted all the gruesome details.

Wet and cloudy. Had kit inspection and found many articles missing, particularly iron rations. As I knew these had been discarded to make room for souvenirs, I dished out some CB to twenty men, which did not hurt them any. Had an open-air concert in the evening.

July 22: From Orlencourt we marched to Hermin, thence to Rebreuve where we billeted for the night. Rebreuve is HQ for the 4th Army. Their staff occupy fine billets. Lieut. Cameron and I invited to dine with "Q" branch of the 4th Army Staff. They were very hospitable and gave us the best dinner we have had in France. Good of them to share their luxury with the PBI (Poor Bloody Infantrymen). After a night's billet at Rebreuve we marched back to Hermin, two miles away, and took over billets from the 1st KRR. This was Major Temple's own regiment, and he was full of pride at meeting them. But they left their billets in a very dirty condition. I was given notice at inspection today that an award of Military Cross is being given to me!

July 23: This afternoon the battalion marched to the Olhain Chateau where we had a general inspection by GOC 4th Army, Gen. Sir Charles Munro, KCB, psc. The 103rd (my) brigade was drawn up in a hollow square when the GOC arrived about 4 p.m. and inspected all ranks. Then three officers were paraded in front of the brigade. Brig. Gen. White of the 4th Army Corps read out the names of the officers and men with a brief account of what each had done to merit the award. My name was included and something said about my work on July 1st. Gen. Munro pinned a ribbon on each man, shook hands, and said a few words to each. He seemed a very nice, sensible old gentleman, and quite human.

After the presentation the party which had been decorated took their place alongside the General at the saluting point and shared with him the general salute from the brigade which marched past. There were lots of congratulations from everyone later for my receiving the Military Cross, and although I was very proud of this honour, I really felt sufficiently rewarded to be still alive and unhurt when so many had fallen on that terrible day.

July 24: Found CSM Welch drunk and incapable when on duty. Worried about him in the trenches tomorrow. Told the RSM to put him under arrest.

July 25: To the trenches on Vimy Ridge early this morning. Met guides from 142nd Infantry Brigade who took us behind Souchez and the hill call Notre Dame de Lorette. Went round the sector occupied by 'B' Company, 24th London Regiment. These are territorials and seemed very casual and slipshod. Saw lots of officers and men half-dressed and without weapons. Walked back to Villers-au-Bois and rode on horse to Hermin alone. A draft of 196 men, reinforcements from Britain, arrived today—some conscripts amongst them—first of that species.

July 27: Got ready to go into the trenches on Vimy Ridge tonight. Transport accompanied us as far as Souchez carrying trench equipment and rations. There was one cart for the entire battalion officers, except for three of the HQ who had a whole cart to themselves. This HQ cart was laden with bedding, wines, and luxuries. The CO (Temple) believes in his own comfort regardless of the rest of his battalion. We left our billets (now at Servins) for the six-mile march to Souchez. Very dark. Souchez is just a collection of stones and brick, which once were buildings. But the cellars are all occupied, many underground shelters. We loaded with rations at Souchez, crossed the duck boards to the foot of Vimy Ridge and relieved the 24th London TF Regt. at 1:30 a.m. Quiet night, fortunately.

July 28: A quiet day on Vimy Ridge. The German trenches are quite close to ours in places. The ground in front is so broken up by shell holes and craters that it is hard to distinguish the trenches from the craters. During the day several Germans showed themselves and shouted across to our men. They evidently knew about our coming into the line last night as enquiries were made about Newcastle (our battalion depot). This knowledge of our whereabouts is a mystery, unless the London Regt. we relieved had been talking over the telephone and were heard by the German microphone. Not a shot was fired on our sector all day. More than half our men were new—in the line for the first time—and had to be told everything. I overheard one of them asking 'Sergeant, where will I find my bed?' These men could be a danger in their ignorance if the sector were aggressive. The rest of the men, survivors of the Somme push, were weary and fed-up. So if the Boche wanted peace and quiet, they were quite agreeable. Probably the Germans have weak and weary units opposite us, similar to our own. In the circumstances this is fortunate—though HQ have not heard of it yet. Too good to last.

Fine and warm. Some of our men stripped and bathed in a stream behind the Ridge within 100 yards of the front line, but out of sight and quite sheltered.

The front lines run along the top of the Ridge. There are support and old abandoned trenches on the slope, which has been fought over fiercely. One hundred and fifty thousand French casualties alone in the summer of 1915. Their bones and equipment are in evidence everywhere. The hill behind us, Notre Dame de Lorette, is still garrisoned by French artillery, who having got their guns up there with difficulty, cannot get them down again. The slope of this hill is dotted with the corpses of Germans—who have made many attempts to take it.

In the evening I was ordered to return to the Servins billets to bring out a draft of men. After dark walked the duckboards to Souchez. These duckboards are the only way of crossing the marsh and stream behind the Ridge. They are sprayed by machine-guns at night at regular intervals. I had to make my way in between these bursts to cross. From Souchez I rode three miles on a bicycle in the dark, then found my horse coming to meet me and went on him back to the transport lines.

No sign of anyone. Went on to Fresnicourt HQ to find out where my draft was. There was no one in. Back again in the afternoon and given tea by the Brigadier and his staff and told I had been sent out of the trenches in error. There are no reinforcements for the 25th. Returned to the transport lines to await orders. Very hot weather.

Aug 1: Still in the transport lines. Hear that Major Temple was carried from the trenches last night with a severe case of gout. Wonder if this is a result of his high living. Quite an example of the hardship endured by this battalion CO who would take in a load of wines and luxuries at the expense of others. Rode over to the field hospital to take some letters to him. He did not seem glad to see me, and I certainly did not enjoy the visit. Feel that retribution for his selfishness has overtaken him.

Made arrangements for a Field General Court Martial on CSM Major Welch, whom I placed under arrest on July 24th. I gave evidence as a witness that he was drunk on duty in the field. There were two other men tried by the same court. Lieuts. Lambert and Wright came out of the trenches to give evidence in Welch's case and gave me news of the battalion. Having lots of trouble with the new men who had been drafted to us. (Welch was later reduced to a sergeant as a result of the court martial)

Aug 8: Ordered to attend a gas school for the past four days. Six officers and twenty NCO's. Part of the course was marching on the double in gas helmets—difficult but can be done. Then put through a gas chamber where chlorine gas was turned on us for twenty-five minutes. Disagreeable, but no harm done through our ordinary PH helmets. Another day we were put through three kinds of gas, with goggles on, plus PH helmets and box respirators. My boots, buttons, etc., were all discoloured, and my clothing smelled so strongly that I had to change to the skin afterward. Have been instructed to return to my battalion.

Aug 11:   In billets at Villers-au-Bois. Major Temple just back from hospital and extremely irritable. He ought to go on sick-leave but obviously afraid if he did he would lose his command. There was a concert tonight by a troupe known as the "Folies." These men are professional artists drawn from the 37th Division, and they give an excellent variety show indeed. Show put on in a big barn and crowded with an enthusiastic audience of officers and men. Our guns firing in the immediate vicinity sometimes drowned out the performers.

Aug 24:   We are now in billets about twelve miles west of Armentieres. Lots of training going on as we get ready for another push. We are badly handicapped for experienced officers and NCO's. I miss the friends who disappeared on the Somme. Told to be ready to move on the 26th. Lots of mystery as to where we are going. Everyone served with new gas helmets, and all equipment inspected and brought up to mark. All unfit men sent away to other depots, along with surplus stores and equipment.

Aug 31:   The mystery of where the push is to be is over. We are back in the Somme area. Our trenches are south of the ruins of Martinpuich. These are new trenches, not made to withstand artillery. It is the line of the last push and marks our farthest advance to date. (Martinpuich is about six miles NE of La Boisselle where the big mines were set off on July 1st) These trenches are not revetted, no duckboards and no room to pass except for bays dug out for passing places. Heavy rains have put things in a terrible state. Considerable heavy shelling going on.

We came up by platoons at 4 a.m. this morning, carrying no packs, but are equipped for trench assault. Heavily shelled this afternoon and evening—expected one to land on me at every moment. Scattered the men in pairs. There are Australians on our left, they were relieved today by Canadians—the first Canadian troops I've met since leaving Canada. The Canadians were also badly shelled, and I loaned them some stretchers for their wounded.

Sept 1:   We were relieved about 5 a.m. by "C" Company, 24th NF. Very glad indeed to get away from the horrible trenches and the heavy shelling. Marched by platoons in small parties to the "D" area which is the old German second line, now used by us as a reserve and rest area. There are splendid deep dugouts in this line, one of these dugouts had been a field hospital—a huge underground chamber with thirty beds, operating room, and dispensary, plus an inclined shaft with rails and frames for lowering loaded stretchers. Spent the day resting in these dugouts.

This part of the Somme has had attacks going on continuously since our push on July 1st, and the enemy are slowly being driven back in a series of minuscule advances, using heavy artillery preparations. The cost in men has been stupendous.

Sept 2: Went to reconnoitre the reserve trenches we go into tomorrow. In the afternoon visited La Boisselle and the place where I lay under fire for those fifteen hours on July 1st. The spot was just in front of the big mine crater at "Y" s.a.p. (commonly called 'saps.' The expression was a corruption of a French phrase meaning 'an undermining' and referred to the small tunnels which went out from the front lines towards the enemy positions). It is a huge crater. Looking from the Boche trenches at the spot where I lay out so long it seems a marvel that I was not hit by the German riflemen and machine-gunners. No wonder my clothing was punctured and bullets dusted me, for I must have been visible. I leaned over the German parapet and took aim at my old position in front and thanked heaven for the rotten marksmanship of Fritz.

The trenches and dugouts at La Boisselle are wonderful. Deep and quite safe. No wonder the Germans were able to hold out there for ten days. The bombardment did not hurt them. Bombs and bayonets did the work in the end after their communications were cut.

Sept 4: Heavy shelling on our front and on both sides. We are making demonstrations—pretending to attack each day, with minor and major attacks twice a week. So the enemy is kept on the jump. He retaliates with promiscuous shelling which is taking a steady toll. Several gas shells fell near us this morning, but we were watching for them and put on the gas masks and had no casualties. There was a push on our left yesterday near Thiepval and the heaviest shelling heard since July 1st.

There was a strong German retaliation, and many of the 24th and 27th were injured. Quite a lot of shells dropped near us—gas shells as well as explosives.

Sept 5: Sent off platoons at ten minute intervals to relieve the 27th NF in the front lines, where they have been heavily shelled. The lines were wiped out as well as the communications trenches in places. Only one platoon got up in time. The others were lost and could not find the platoons they were to relieve. I had to take them in myself one after another, and we were consequently very late. With green officers and NCO's and no guides, such delay could not be helped as I could only take in one at time then go back through the mud and shell holes for another. Raining, cold, and miserable. Tired out and covered with mud. I scattered the company in a series of shell holes, organized the strong points where every little party was on its own.

Then the CO (Temple) sent for me, and I had to trudge back nearly two miles to battalion HQ where I was dressed down for the delay in this morning's relief. A most unjust and unreasonable procedure in view of the conditions we are operating under, but I suppose it is to be expected from the 'red tabs' far behind the lines in comfortable dugouts. They know little and apparently could care less about the actualities of this terrible war. Plodded back from this unnecessary HQ performance, through the shelling and mud to my shell hole with my company. Nothing to eat or drink. After dark we had to work hard to improve our positions, joining the parties together.

Sept 6:   Shelling lessened for awhile. After dark all worked at linking up strong points. Everyone is tired out and unnerved by the shelling and exposure. No shelters at all. But HQ insists on this extra activity. We were relieved at 6 a.m. and made the changes without casualties. Went back to the reserve trenches near the ruins of Contalmaison and slept like logs until 5 p.m. in the open trench, despite the shelling and noise of our guns. On account of the gas shells the dugouts are unsafe. Big barrage and attack over High Wood on our right. Contalmaison is indistinguishable from the churned-up ground around—just a rubble heap.

One of our men killed by a direct shell hit—shell did not explode. He was sleeping and never knew anything.

Sept 10:   Sent out a covering party last night to protect a working party consolidating new positions gained by the Highlanders at High Wood. Our party ran into a barrage as they were leaving and had heavy casualties—at least two NCO's gone. Canadians on our left suffered a great many casualties during the ensuing German bombardment. Noise from our guns just behind our trench is terrific. Had to get into a deep dugout and risk the gas shells to get some relief. CO Temple sent for me to report to HQ. Took my orderly, McCourt, and passed through the barrage safely. Was ordered to examine and report on an old line to the left of 'Gordon Alley'—and required to 'go at once.' In daylight! Absolute suicide as this old line is under continuous fire—the Germans believing it still occupied, though the Canadians had abandoned it and moved in front. Told the CO this, but he insisted I go anyhow. Incredible!

Left McCourt in Gordon Alley and told him to return and report me missing if I was not back in by dark. Then I crawled over the top and reconnoitred the old line. It was all knocked to pieces and getting steadily worse by the shells which fell on it whilst I went over it. Never expected to return. Miraculously I did, unhurt! Sent in my report— that the line was of no further use. It did not require this unnecessary risk of my life to know this, as it was obvious to anyone watching the shells fall on that position that it could not be occupied.

Sept 11:   The CO Temple sent for me again today, and when I reported to him in HQ, well in the rear of us, safe in a comfortable dugout, I was ordered to reconnoitre the '6th Avenue' trench. I carefully explained to him that this trench, also, which was formerly our front line, had been so badly shelled and strafed that it had to be abandoned as it was useless to us. However, the Germans, not apparently aware of this, kept it under constant fire and strafing. It had been practically wiped out and was completely uninhabitable. However, he insisted I go, personally, and—again—in daylight to make a report.

Quite unexpectedly I again returned safely—which I can only credit to unbelievable luck under the conditions which I encountered. Made my report. After the experiences of yesterday and today it is obvious that this CO puts no value whatsoever on his men's lives. To be asked to risk one's life for a purpose is one thing, but for something like this—a useless and unnecessary operation—makes one question the power given to those who make decisions for so many when they know so little. Not once has this CO been nearer to the front than the battalion HQ, which is always a long way back. He knows nothing of the conditions his men and officers are enduring, and from his attitude, one judges he really does not care.

Sept 16:   About three thousand prisoners taken in the push yesterday which captured Courcelette, Martinpuich, and Flers. Our planes are up in force. They brought down nine balloons and twelve Boche planes.

In the advance of yesterday we saw tanks for the first time. Ungainly monsters. We had heard rumours of a new weapon, very hush-hush, to counteract the terrible machine-guns which so devastate our lines. These great machines lumbered along, and they certainly were impervious to machine-guns. The big problem was to keep them from becoming mired. And there are pitifully few of them—someone had said perhaps only forty or fifty. It was some sight to see them crawling along, over barbed-wire, and across trenches, then right up to those lethal machine-gun nests—and over them!

But I will never forget one episode. Behind one of the ridges a number of corpses (our own men) lay—almost in a pile—when they had been mowed down by the machine-guns. Over the top of this ridge came a tank, crushing the bodies like matchwood right there, parts of the bodies splayed out around the thing. And it came to rest at that particular point, obviously unbeknown to the driver. In this war of dreadful, gruesome happenings, this experience almost finished me off.

Oct 1:   Left the Somme area on 20th Sept and now in the Armentieres region again. This is the front line which I am holding with four NCO's, twenty-four men, two Lewis guns, and one Vickers machine-gun. An equal number of men are in support trenches behind me. Fairly quiet at the moment.

Oct 2:   Still quiet, so the CO came round today. As is usual when these birds appear, it is always safe and quiet. Went round the trenches with him and learned the details of the next push—whenever it comes.

Oct 8:   Was ordered to proceed to Etaples (on the coast) tomorrow for a period of duty as an instructor at the base. A great surprise to me as I had been given no warning, even though the CO must have been aware. Since I am the superior captain of the battalion it seems he might have had the decency to advise me—but no matter, it will be a welcome change.

Oct 12:   In training camp Number 2, near Etaples, south of Boulogne. All reinforcements from Britain, via Boulogne, come to this training camp, known throughout the army as the Bull Ring, for intensive training under instructors from the front lines—officer and NCO's. One per division is sent here to instruct for two months. The CO is Major Lamb, 2nd NF. He is strict and energetic.

Oct 15:   Had this afternoon off, so walked to Etaples from camp and took the train to Le Touquet Paris Plage, about six miles away, out on the coast. Had tea there and walked back. It is thirteen years since my last visit to Le Touquet when I worked in the resort for Sir Henry Curtis. Many fine buildings around—very different from when I last saw it. Walked part way home through the woods with Johnson, my RND tent mate, and Capt. Haulin, 2nd Rifle Brigade.

Have had a few good games of bridge in the evenings in camp. There are some excellent players, including Lieut. de la Rue, who has written a book on auction bridge and is an expert. His battalion of the London Regiment has been wiped out, and he is here indefinitely.

Nov 23: Still acting as training instructor at Number 2 training camp near Etaples—the Bull Ring. The weather has been awful for the past month, heavy rain, gales, and icy winds. Tents are the only shelter, and it is impossible to get dry in them in this cold, wet weather. My blankets and overcoat have been damp for weeks. Had a parcel today from Meta which included some warm clothing and new breeches. They were dry and most welcome.

Nov 30: Training as usual in the Bull Ring. Very cold winds. Hard work to keep the troops interested—their minds are concentrated on their cold and misery. Bitterly cold in our tents at night. It takes a long time to get warm enough to sleep. I have been fighting off a cold for several weeks, sore throat, etc. Seems impossible to get rid of it in these conditions. Am to see the MO tomorrow.

Dec 2: Hospitalized. Pneumonia.''

This was the last entry in the little notebook Trevor had carried with him through the battlefields of France. When he was able to travel he was sent to Britain to recuperate and was in Swansea on January 19, 1917, when he had a notification from Buckingham Palace stating: "Your attendance is required on January 24th at 11 a.m. in service dress to be invested with the award of the Military Cross." It was signed by the Lord Chamberlain of London. And a telegram from the War Office followed advising him that his leave had been extended to January 25th to permit him to attend the above investiture.

When he reported for duty following the ceremony his health was classified as B1, and he was seconded to the Royal Flying Corps (later to be called the RAF), first to the 98th squadron, then later to the night-bombing 83rd squadron as station adjutant and recording officer. Based in London, the 83rd also had a balloon section. His organizational capabilities together with active service experience enabled him to make a valuable contribution. Although in the course of his duties he often ascended in the air over the vicinity of the front line, he never again returned to the trenches.

Meta brought Jackie to London, and they rented a flat at 26, York Mansions, Prince of Wales Road in Battersea.

The notebook was laid to rest along with the MC. Over the years the nightmare memories associated with these two articles may have eased with the passage of time. But Trevor, like others who had also served in those blood-soaked trenches, found that it was a trauma which could only be talked about with the men who had been through the same ordeal.

FIFTEEN

THE YEAR OF 1916 HAD come to an end, but still the war ground on and casualty lists continued to be staggering. Perhaps the German Prince Max Bader echoed the thoughts of most participants when he wrote: "There is bitter and complete disillusionment all round. We and our enemies have shed our best blood by the torrent, yet neither they nor we are one step nearer to victory, and there is no prospect in sight other than further terrible battles and useless slaughter." And 1917 certainly brought more of that. In the battle for Passchendaele, Britain alone lost over 245 thousand men and Douglas Haig gained a bare five miles of shell-pocked, bloody mire. There were other similar disasters. Yet the front line changed very little.

Then in April of 1917, the United States, angered by the sinking of some of her ships by the Germans, declared war on Germany and her allies and began fielding an army to send to France. The first American troops arrived in August of 1917, but it was 1918 before the main force got into the battle. At last the deadlock was broken. The arrival of fresh, eager American soldiers pouring in at a rate of three hundred thousand a month turned the tide, and on November 11, 1918, an armistice was signed. The scenes which followed the news that the war was at last over ranged from wild jubilation in most centres, to disbelief on the part of some of the dazed, exhausted soldiers still in the trenches.

In London the crowds went mad with delight and staged a huge parade in Trafalgar Square. Trevor took Jackie, now seven, with him to watch as regiments and bands, all in their full-dress uniforms, marched by. The Allies were well-represented. As they watched, Trevor was suddenly swept by dizziness and felt so ill he wondered if he would be able to get his son safely home. He was barely in the door of their flat when he collapsed.

Meta, four months pregnant with their second child, had been feeling queasy that day, so had not gone with them. But the sight of Trevor crumpled on the floor brought her instantly to her feet in alarm. Frantically she telephoned for a doctor.

This gentleman took one look at Trevor, made a few tests, then told Meta tersely, "He's got influenza and he's a very sick man. He must go into hospital immediately." When told of this Trevor begged to be allowed to stay at home, but the doctor wanted no part of home visits. "We are rushed off our feet already with the ever-increasing number of flu' patients. Its all I can do to handle my hospital cases," he told them. "Besides," he warned Trevor, "your wife is in no condition to cope with the round-the-clock care you are going to need—and every available nurse is already working, so there would be no one at all to help out here."

In hospital Trevor grew rapidly worse, and it seemed obvious he was dying. With grossly over-crowded wards and a medical staff already seriously strained to the limit—a situation worsening by the hour as doctors, nurses, and other hospital staff also succumbed to the illness—emergency methods were in effect. Hard decisions had to be made as to the best use of the few hands available. Patients for whom no hope whatsoever was entertained simply had to be left to the care of a Higher Power, so that all available earthly care could be given to those with some chance of recovery.

Thus Trevor was rammed into a tiny ward with twenty-four

other men, also dying. He was vaguely aware of death services being read, then lost all idea of time as he drifted in and out of consciousness.

Because of Meta's pregnancy her doctor absolutely forbade her to go near the place, and she had to rely on Gwilym for reports. Gwilym did not dare to tell her that Trevor was not expected to live and faithfully visited each day—expecting the worst every time he went. The comatose Trevor rarely knew Gwilym had been to see him. But despite Gwilym's carefully worded reports, Meta began intuitively to sense all was not well after a few weeks. She became so concerned she decided one day to defy all orders and was just leaving the flat to find out exactly what was happening when Gwilym came bounding up the stairs.

He hugged her impulsively. "He's done it!" he cried half sobbing. "Can't believe it...he's in terrible shape, but he's alive, and he's conscious. It's like a miracle..." He sank into a chair as they reentered the flat. "God! Meta...I never thought he'd pull through. He's shockingly weak...but he's going to make it."

It was a shell of a man who came home eventually, haggard, skeleton-thin, with chalk-coloured cheeks—so frail Meta's heart sank. He couldn't walk alone, but strong arms carried him into the flat. "Give him a week or so," Gwilym suggested, "then if I were you, I'd take him to Cornwall for the winter. This London climate is no place to convalesce."

Later Gwilym told her that of the twenty-four men put into that death ward with Trevor in the London hospital, two had miraculously survived—Trevor and a big Australian doctor. The others had all died, their beds soon filled with more doomed flu' victims as the epidemic reached the height of its devastating rampage.

With Gwilym's help Meta took Trevor to Looe in Cornwall, a place not only with a kinder climate, but also with happy memories, as this was where he had proposed to her—so many years ago, before going off to South America.

As his health slowly improved Trevor longed to return to Canada. "How I would love to be back there again," he told Meta. "Don't think I could ever fit in here again...didn't like it much before and it's no better now. How about you, Luv? How do you feel?" Meta looked at this husband she had so nearly lost. She was worried that his convalescence seemed to be taking longer than anticipated. Perhaps the freedom and peace of his beloved Island might be the spark to revive the old vitality so much a part of Trevor. "I can be ready to go anytime you say," she told him. "Perhaps it would do us all good to have a complete change of scene."

When she had returned to Swansea at the beginning of the war, it had been so wonderful to see her family again that she had hoped they could remain when Trevor's service was through. But during the past five years there had been many changes. Her adored father had died suddenly in the spring of 1917, her brothers and sisters were now all married and away in homes of their own. Strathmore, the Taylor home in Mumbles, had been sold, and Molly Taylor (Meta's step-mother) was living in a Golders Green flat in London.

The same was true of Trevor's family—even more so, for many of his family had gone to the far corners. Graham, now married, was in Malaya, and Harold was in India. Gladys, also married and now home with her two children, might be going back with her husband to South Africa. Gwilym was in London with his wife, but talking of moving. Only Gwennie, the eldest of the family, was still at home in Swansea. Morgan and Rachel Williams had sold Troed-y-bryn and moved to a small flat in the Sketty district of Swansea. Most of their friends were similarly scattered and many, including dear Hart Jenkins, had been lost in the terrible war. Life could never be the same. Trevor, still in uniform but now classified as a C1 healthwise, reported back for duty in the spring of 1919 and applied for repatriation to Canada. However, getting back to Canada was not as easy as making the decision to go. Huge crowds of people besieged the ticket offices as long lines of demobilized soldiers, wives, and wives-to-be clamoured for reservations on the few ships left for civilian traffic. After weeks of searching and standing in line, Trevor could only find two vacancies—one on a ship leaving in late March of 1919 and the other six months later in September. With a baby due early in April, the March sailing was out of the question, so they had to be content with the September booking.

In the meantime he was posted to No. 4 (Chelsea) Aircraft Repair Depot as the Depot Adjutant, handling administration for eighteen hundred men and 120 officers as this station was gradually phased out. From here he was sent to No. 2 Group Concentration Camp at Uxbridge before going later to the RAF camp at Winchester. After many queries he learned that he was to be granted a disability pension for one year after he landed in Canada. It would total about thirty-five pounds for the entire year. "Oh, well," he remarked, "I suppose it is better than nothing at all, but that's the best you can say for such a decision."

"How would you like to have your baby in a millionaire's home?" Meta's doctor asked as time for her confinement approached. "Pierpont Morgan has turned his mansion at 13 Princes Gate in Kensington over to the British Government to be used as a maternity hospital for the wives of servicemen, and I'd like to book you in there."

When Trevor went to visit her following the birth of their daughter on April 9th, he found Meta luxuriating in the magnificent surroundings, the best of everything, including priceless paintings, statuary, furniture, drapes, and carpeting. "Some difference from Jackie's arrival," he remarked, remembering the tar-paper shack in Massett, coal-oil lamps, and two mid-wives who assisted the entry of that young man into the world. "It's wonderful," agreed Meta. "Thank goodness for kind-hearted millionaires who share their opulence. I intend to revel in every moment of my stay here." The baby, named Kathleen Elizabeth by her parents, was promptly called "Betty" by her eight-year-old brother, in honour of a tomboy-ish nine-year-old he liked to play with. But like most small boys, Jackie was very disillusioned by the scrap of a morsel all the adults were making such a fuss over and on whom he had bestowed the name of his favourite chum. "Sure is small," was his disgusted comment when he saw his sister for the first time.

In September the long-awaited return trip to Canada had to be postponed. They had been booked to leave on the 15th, but Jackie, who had been eating green apples snitched from a forbidden tree, developed a bad stomach-ache which went on for a little too long. Upon taking him to a hospital, it was found that green apples weren't the only problem—he had a ruptured appendix. He was a pretty sick little boy and was kept in hospital for nine weeks before being released, still weak and shaky.

At last, on October 31st of 1919, the Williams family boarded the SS *Baltic* for the trip across the Atlantic. This crossing was uneventful—even the weather was kind. The new baby, seven months old, was comfortably bedded in a steamer trunk for the voyage and slept most of the time. Jackie, now recovered, was a different proposition. It took both of his parents to keep track of him—he was off into so many places on board ship with all the energy and curiosity of a healthy eight-year-old.

They arrived in Prince Rupert on the transcontinental train only to learn they had missed the fortnightly boat to Masset Inlet by a day, so there was nothing for it but to put up in a hotel and wait. They were both wondering what they would find when they eventually did reach home. How would the log house have fared for these past five years. They had heard there was no one at all living in Graham Centre, most of the bachelors having gone into the forces and many families having either left the Islands or—as in the case of the Rennies and John McDougall—moved to Port Clements.

"Perhaps it might be a good idea for us to rent a place in Port Clements for the first while," Trevor suggested. "Jackie will need to go to school, and it will only be a few years before Betty will also be ready. We'll hang on to the preemption though, and if it looks as though we can manage to live there, we can always move back. But the cabin is bound to need a lot of repairs after so many years. And I will have to find some sort of work. . . ."

Meta nodded. "Yes," she agreed, "it might be a good idea—give us a chance to get our bearings, and Port Clements is so close it will almost feel like going home."

Obtaining a job was to be the easiest of Trevor's projects. While waiting for the *Prince Albert* to take them to Masset Inlet, Trevor took Jackie out for walks each day and on one such outing saw a poster nailed to a pole saying that several positions as Forest Rangers were open for any returned men who could pass the exams. He went to a local sawmill to check out some lumber statistics and so on, took the exam, and passed easily.

The position he was offered as a result was as assistant ranger for Masset Inlet with his base to be in Port Clements. Although disappointed that returning to preemption life at this time was not practical, the job as forest ranger was at least a fair substitution. It would mean being out in the open and travelling to various places around the region—not stuck in an office, a situation he had come to dread as a way of life.

This time Meta and Trevor did not have to take the steamer to Masset, then transfer to a small launch for the rest of the trip home. Now the *Prince Albert* took them the entire way, docking at the government wharf Herb Clements had been instrumental in securing for Eli's town. And what a booming little town met their eyes!

From a hamlet of only a few families when they had left in 1914, it was now home to over one thousand residents with another five to six hundred in the surrounding area. Three sawmills were operating full blast, one on either side of the government wharf and a third on the old Barton site. There was also an annex to the government wharf which was piled high with lumber and bustling with activity. Across the Inlet to the west was another big mill in the recently named Buckley Bay. The *Albert* stopped in Buckley Bay en route to Port Clements and it appeared a hive of industry also. Besides these four mills there was still another sawmill—in Sewall, near Ship Island. And in the general area of Masset Inlet and its adjoining Juskatla Inlet there were thirteen or fourteen busy logging camps all getting out the famed aeroplane spruce, which was being bought up as soon as it could be supplied. With the war over that market would soon be coming to an end—in fact, by the end of November one mill, the operation on the Barton site, did shut down, and one by one the others eventually followed. But not for a few years.

Graham Centre, as expected, was abandoned—weather and thieves having reduced the houses to little more than shells. It was a depressing sight. Their own house had suffered a similar fate—there was very little left. The door hung open, and obviously cattle had been using the house during inclement weather. No one seemed to know what had happened to their belongings. When Charlie Adam had enlisted for overseas service in 1916, he had given the key to someone who subsequently also enlisted, and nothing much was known of events following this. Evidently it must have been presumed the Williams' wouldn't return, and it was a help-yourself situation. Bill Rennie said he had looked in now and again, then on one trip found someone had been there and removed most of the books, pictures, and other smaller objects. Shortly after this the larger pieces of furniture, rugs, and so on were gone. The door was left open, and wandering cattle made it a barn of sorts. "There are so many newcomers in the place now," Rennie said. "An awful lot of riff-raff. We've had damage to our place in Graham Centre, too, in spite of the fact that I'm keeping a sharp eye out for this."

In addition to the vandalism the war years had taken a toll of life from the Graham Centre area. The two Jims, McLay and Allison, who had built the log house on the ridge behind the Williams', had both been killed in France, as had young Arthur Richardson, who had lived near the store. And of course dear Hart Jenkins, who had been lost in the Somme bloodbath on July 1, 1916, would never return. Thomas O'Callaghan had joined up, been severely wounded and, unfit for preemption life, had gone to live nearer medical assistance in a more populated place. Geordie McQuaker in his own way was also a war casualty. His extreme melancholia when he was rejected for military service had created such a feeling of depression in this fiercely patriotic man that he would live out his life in a mental institution. Charlie Adam, the feisty owner of the townsite, now realized his town would never be. He, too, had been wounded in the war and lost two brothers at Vimy. "I'll not be back," he had written Trevor. "Too many changes. My energy for townsiting is gone." Instead, Charlie went to Stewart and acquired a Ford Motor agency which he ran for many years before moving to Terrace, where he built a movie theatre—and got married. In later years he and his wife

A section of Port Clements 1920. About 1000 to 1500 people made their homes in the small town. This photo shows three mills in operation: A–the Nadeau mill (formerly Barton's); B–the Lynch mill and C–the Lewis mill. Under the dotted lines are 1–Bert Tingley's Yakoun Hotel and 2–the GWVA under construction.

Photo believed to have been taken by Charles Graham and made into a postcard.

The Lynch Mill in operation. Ran until the late 1920s. Remains of the cement foundation under the engine and boiler-room may still be seen (1989) near the Yakoun Pub.

Photo—Alice McCrea

Planked street in Port Clements was built by Nadeau during World War One, so that the lumber could be moved to the main government dock more easily. Under the dotted line is Bill Hastie's building with dance hall upstairs and pool room down. Beside it is his bakery, also used as a store for some years. The GWVA is in the centre of the photo. It also had a dance hall upstairs. Fence on extreme right encloses Bert Tingley's fine garden, protected from village cows.
Photo–Mrs. Edith Dyson

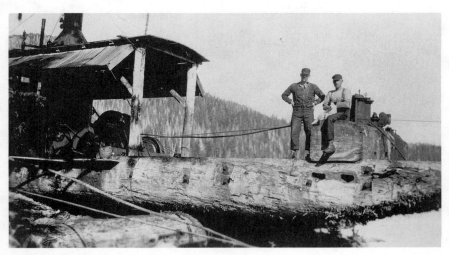

Early-day wood-fired steam donkey and sled. Man on the left wears the typical garb of that day, trousers known as "bone-drys," also called "tin pants" because the material was so stiff.
Photo–George McRae

moved to Tsawwassen.

It was difficult to find a house in the overcrowded Port Clements of 1919 and early 1920s. Meta and Trevor rented a variety of places for two years before finding a suitable home to buy—the former house and office of Imperial Munitions Board agent, Cooper Young, on the hill next door to their pioneering neighbours, Eli and Ruth Tingley.

They were still in one of the rented houses when they had a visit from another old friend, Dave Tuft. "Just heard you were back, T.L.," said Dave, calling Trevor by the nickname most commonly given him locally. "Wanted to let you know I've got some of your pictures and other small items stashed away at my Striae Island cabin. I heard your place had been broken into and people stealing things, so I brought my boat over and gathered up what I could for you. It's a damn shame. Can't leave homes the way we used to any more. Never said anything to anyone about having your stuff for fear they might ransack my place too. I don't know—lots of strange people came in with the mills, and they don't seem to know how to behave...I was pretty disgusted, I can tell you. To go into a person's home and steal like that..." He shook his head in a gesture of utter condemnation.

Meta could have hugged him. How thoughtful and kind he had been to go to all that trouble—the pictures and other items he had salvaged for them had been carefully wrapped and well-looked after, undoubtedly in much better condition than had they been left for so many years in an unheated log home—never mind the fact of vandals or that cattle had been using their place as a stop-over. Mr. Tuft, a quiet intellectual man of simple tastes, had two homesteads, both well away from too much contact with civilization. One was near Striae Island, north of the old Haida village of Yan, on the opposite side of the Sound from Old Masset, and another about five or six miles south of Port Clements, along the Skid Road.

He had been staying in the latter when a visitor dropped by and told him of the Williams' return. "I'm the only one of the homesteaders left down that way, now," he said, referring to the seventeen or eighteen homesites which had been occupied by pioneers in the Skid Road—Centre Meridian area from 1909 to 1918. "At least five of them went off to the war—Jack Wilson, Daniels, Thomas, Harry Ross, and Fred Chapman. I heard that Wilson and Daniels were killed in France. But both Ross and Chapman are back from the war, and they're living in Port now. Maxwell, another of the homesteaders, also lives in Port. Gave up preemption life to work for the Tingleys.

"Anyhow, gradually everyone left except me—I still like it out there and go back for a time each year. Can't have the same kind of garden I do out at Striae, though, so I usually spend my summers there when I'm not out on a cooking job."

The Centre Meridian he referred to was a survey line which ran from the north end of Township 14, between lots 15 and 16, due south to Queen Charlotte City. A trail from the outskirts of Port Clements ran at an angle to connect with it, and it was the main means of access for the homesteaders who lived adjacent to it. It was about ¾ of a mile to the east of the Skid Road which paralleled it for about six miles. The Skid Road was the roughly slashed route over which Wright and Green had taken their coal drilling equipment into the Wilson Creek area in 1911. Homesteads had been taken up by preemptors south and east of Port Clements for five miles in the proximity of the Skid Road and the Centre Meridian trail

As Meta and Trevor gradually settled into the community life in Port Clements, Meta was asked to be the organist for the weekly church services. She was practicing hymns one afternoon when she noticed the altar covering was hanging askew. It bothered her to see it this way, and she went to adjust the cloth. In lifting the skirt to even the hem, she got it a little too high on one side. When she bent to make the correction she caught sight of a pile of books underneath the altar. They looked awfully familiar. Puzzled, she took one out and sure enough, there on the fly leaf was her name. Taking more, she found that the books were all theirs—some fifty or more. How they came to be under the altar no one seemed to know. Nor did they ever find out. But there was their library, almost intact. Perhaps someone had felt as Dave Tuft had and had decided that the books should be put in safe-keeping, and this was the perfect hiding place.

SIXTEEN

OF THE ONE HUNDRED and twenty men known to have enlisted from the north end of Graham Island in the 1914–1918 war, very few came back. Too many lay in unmarked graves in France. Others, suffering from the effects of the war, decided to make a fresh start elsewhere, the vigour of youth which had precipitated the pioneering venture in the wilds now lost.

For those who did return to the area, they were back in one piece for the most part and wanted nothing more than to put the horrors of the war behind them. All were in various stages of trauma from the unspeakable condition of the trenches, the nightmare sight of those bloody heaps of khaki strewn everywhere after the pushes, the excruciating barbed wire and noise and din of the big guns. Some still bore the visible signs of the conflict such as the gassings, shell-shock, and wounds. They were a small band among the numerous people now actively pursuing life in the community and round-about. An atmosphere of elation and high spirits seemed to prevail. On weekends loggers from the surrounding camps would pour into Port Clements, overflowing the few dance halls and pool rooms and so on that existed—people who had known nothing of the realities of the war.

Those who had come back from it felt a need to draw together, not to discuss what had happened—no one wanted that. To a man they ached to put the memories to rest, but they needed a buffer of some sort before they could enter the mainstream again. When someone suggested, "Let's build a club house," the idea took off immediately. No doubt the psychiatrists of today can explain how a catharsis and eventual healing began as walls were erected and floors laid. The hammering of nails was therapeutic, and a project of building together was irresistible.

But they wanted an organization. So on November 1, 1919, the first meeting of the Graham Island Branch of the Great War Veterans Association was held and was commonly known thereafter as the GWVA. R.P. Ponder was elected president; George Mayer and L. Richter, 1st and 2nd vice-presidents; C.W.A. Drader, secretary-treasurer; Ralph Stafford, sergeant-at-arms; Arthur Robertson, Wes and Eddy Singer, executive committee; and Felix Graham, auditor. With the exception of Ponder and Drader, all were pioneers of the northern area of Graham Island. Ponder, an ex-serviceman, was the newly-appointed police constable for the north end, and Drader, an ex-army lieutenant, taught the one-roomed school with its eight grades in Port Clements. Trevor joined the organization as soon as he returned later that same month, as did some thirty others, to make an eventual membership of thirty-six to thirty-eight, which naturally fluctuated as men came and went from the district.

Most of the members lived in Port Clements, but they did have veterans from Tlell as well as New Masset and even one Haida, Albert Edwards from Old Masset, who showed up fairly regularly.

The idea which had begun modestly enough as a simple club room was soon enlarged to include a dance hall upstairs, with club and dressing rooms downstairs, and a sizeable space, also downstairs, to rent out to provide some income. Lumber, fittings, and like material were delivered to the site with promises to pay later, and the big building was mainly constructed by the members themselves without pay. Money was borrowed, mostly from the members, and by April of 1920 an active Women's Auxiliary to the GWVA had raised the down-payment for a player piano. Now they could hold the dances and entertainments in their own building—the roof was on and floor laid. Soon the place echoed with the music of the era, two-steps, turkey-trots, waltzes, and a new fad—the Charleston.

In later years Trevor would recall particularly the efforts of C.W.A. Drader. "He was an excellent school teacher, yet always seemed to have plenty of time for his other energetic pursuits, amongst which was a prime interest in promoting and building the GWVA (building). In fact it was mainly due to him that the ambitious place was finished. He worked on it after school and on weekends continuously, with an enthusiasm which was infectious."

By the mid to late 1920s the population dwindled as mills closed. Money became scarce and creditors pressed. The GWVA branch had no legal standing—could not own nor dispose of property. An emergency meeting was held and Trevor elected secretary-treasurer with full authority to try to clear up the difficulties. "The thought that all our work might be lost and our good name tarnished was unthinkable," he said when discussing the event in later years. "With help from some of the remaining vets, the United Services Society was formed, incorporated, and registered. Under this name we sold the building to Frank Pearce, who had rented the downstairs from us for the year in 1925. He was running the White Lunch Cafe next door and not doing well as things slackened off. . . wanted to diversify his business. On December 24, 1926, he arranged to buy our building for $2000. Gave us a down-payment at once enabling us to pay off our principal creditors. The balance was paid over a period of two years. By the end of 1929 everyone who had wages due or who had loaned money was paid off in full—a tremendous satisfaction to us all."

Pearce had a bargain. The building which had cost $4389.22 in materials alone—to say nothing of the hundreds of hours in labour—was worth many times what he paid for it. But the vets were too few in number by then to be able to operate it, and with available funds shrinking to almost nil, the sale was an infinite relief to them. Pearce moved in immediately, converted the dance hall upstairs into bedrooms for a hotel, with a store and cafe on the ground floor, and ran the entire establishment on his own until he retired in the early 1940s. During the World War Two years the building was leased by a logging company as a storage and distributing centre for their operation in Juskatla. In subsequent years it was purchased by Ernie and Maureen Chapman who remodeled the place extensively and added a sizeable wing on the west side as they converted it into a more modern general store with living quarters on the second floor.

The first school in Port Clements had opened on June 1st, 1913. Taught by Laura Tingley, it was in session for nineteen days for its initial term. Classes were held in Eli's sixteen by sixteen-foot cabin, and with only eight to ten children to begin with, the place was adequate although primitive. The children approached this school along big cedar logs, flattened on the top side, to which a rather shaky railing had been nailed to keep them from falling off. Occasionally extreme high tides flooded the schoolroom floor, and classes had to be cancelled for that day—to the delight of the pupils.

With the opening of the school it was deemed necessary to appoint three temporary trustees until an official election was held on July 13th to get things in order for the school term beginning in September. Wes Singer, Bill Hastie, and Bert Tingley agreed to act in the interim. An annual report was filed for this interim period showing total expenses incurred were $8 which included $6 for a bookcase and $2 for fuel.

At the first official election Bert Tingley was elected for a term of three years, Walter Cross for two years, and Wes Singer for one year. Albert R. Mallory was elected auditor. It was moved and seconded to ask the Superintendent of Schools to define the boundaries of the school district so that money could be raised by local assessment. Also approved was a motion to notify all the parents in the district that they must send their children to school. Bert Tingley was appointed secretary-treasurer and set the pattern of maintaining an assiduously conscientious record of all expenditures and receipts. One does not find any of the sloppy "miscellaneous" titles in his entries—he knew exactly where each cent went or came from, a practice which was adhered to all during the life of this local school board. Even the most minute expenditure has been recorded. It is interesting to note that for most of those years the project of a school garden was part of the curriculum.

In the early 1930s the local school boards were dissolved and administration took place from Prince Rupert for many years. Finally an all-Islands school board was formed, with trustees from each local area, but never again would each small settlement have its own board, as had been the case initially.

By 1916 there were too many pupils for the log cabin to accommodate, so for the next two years St. Mark's Anglican Church was rented for $6.00 a month and used as a classroom during the weekdays. The tall, willowy Miss Jenks came to teach the youngsters at this point, and was squired to the various community activities by young David Maxwell, who had been one of the Centre Meridian homesteaders prior to moving into Port Clements. Maxie, as he was commonly known, was several inches shorter than Miss Jenks, and Fred Chapman, who was a thirteen-year-old pupil in the school in 1916, recalls that the older pupils seemed to find it side-splittingly funny to see Maxie and the tall Miss Jenks together. Fred and his sister, Louise, both attended the school. Their parents, part of the original Centre Meridian homesteaders, had moved into Port Clements to await the birth of their third child, Ernest. Then when Mr. Chapman returned from subsequent war service overseas, the family decided to make their permanent home in Port Clements.

By 1918 the Port Clements School Board had obtained funds to purchase several lots on the hill behind the church and called for tenders for a proper schoolhouse. Brent Lea was awarded the contract. The new school was built that year and total cost, including $235 for Lea himself, was $1336.44 according to the records of the School Board.

On January 1, 1919, the children were moved to their new classroom. There were forty pupils at that time in grades from one to eight—all in one large room—with one teacher. The following year six more lots were added to give the school a full acre of property. Because of the rainy weather prevalent in this part of the world, the playground was often muddy, so a covered play area in the form of a big wooden building was erected close by the school.

It was into this school, with C.W.A. Drader as teacher, that Jackie Williams went when his parents returned at the end of November 1919. Since Mr. Drader already had two boys named Jack in his classes, he decreed that Jack Williams would henceforth be known as John—at least in school. The name stuck, and from that time on he was Johnny Williams, despite the fact that both the other Jacks left within a relatively short time.

Brent Lea, who had built the school for such a modest sum, spent a busy year in 1918. Not only did he oversee the construction of that building, but he also went to work for the Massett Timber Company, under the managership of Frank L. Buckley, who planned to put in a mill in Port Clements. This would be in addition to the three mills already operating at full capacity there. Buckley put Lea in charge of all construction, and the first item on the agenda was an office-cum-residence for Cooper Young, the Imperial Munitions Board representative. It was built in less than a week. (This was the house purchased by Trevor and Meta Williams in 1922.) This accomplished, Lea was instructed to put up a warehouse and office near the approach to the government wharf for the Massett Timber Company. This was also soon finished. But in discussing the best site for the mill, Brent Lea found the idea of putting such an operation so far from the source of logs impractical, and he persuaded the company to choose a cove on the west side of Masset Inlet—a cove soon given the name of Buckley Bay. Although it became a community in its own right, Buckley Bay nevertheless did feed into Port Clements for supplies to a significant degree.

With the cessation of war on November 11, 1918, the Imperial Munitions Board had no more need for the aeroplane spruce they had been buying—almost with wild abandon— and their agent, Cooper Young was recalled. The Woods family, whose daughter Ruth had married Eli Tingley, bought the Cooper Young house, and, when they left to live in Victoria in 1922, sold it to the Williams'.

Although the Williams family would make their home in this house for the next seventeen years, Trevor always hated the place and never intended to stay in it for more than a short time. He disliked being surrounded so closely by other houses—no privacy to speak of—and dreamed of being able to return to the beloved preemption with room to breathe. However, he was practical enough to realize that the logistics of raising a family beyond walking distance to a school would present too many problems. For the time being, Port Clements would have to do.

He was still with the Forestry Department as Assistant Ranger for the area, travelling about the region first on the *Geraldine R*, then the *Red Cedar*. On these launches he would go as far as Langara Island and Naden Harbour, as well as all around Masset and Juskatla Inlets, calling in at the numerous camps to check on trees being harvested.

On July 7, 1922, another daughter was born to Meta and Trevor. Named Nancy, she came into the world in the home of Mrs. Raybold, a capable nurse living in Delkatla, who was assisted in the delivery by the doctor from Massett. Meta was now forty-two, but the birth went without incident, and the baby was soon home being admired by her older sister and brother. This time John (Jackie) was prepared for a tiny sister who could do little more than look sleepily at him—it was not the shock he had received when Betty was born and he had been expecting a decently-sized playmate.

In the fall of 1923 Trevor was offered a promotion in the Forestry Service if he would accept a transfer to Burns Lake. "Perhaps I'd better go up and see what it's all about before taking you and the children there," he suggested to Meta. Much as she hated to be parted from him, Meta knew this was the sensible thing to do.

It was bitterly cold in Burns Lake that winter, and Trevor nearly froze using the open hand-car on the railroad tracks when he had to travel to some of the outlying places. For duties nearer the town he could use snowshoes—something he hadn't done since his stay in Montreal. Because of the freezing weather, water was extremely scarce, people sometimes paying seventy-five cents for a small barrel. This was too much like the memory of South Africa, and he hated the idea of submitting his family to such a waterless situation.

Soon Trevor would have to decide whether he wanted to make the job permanent. He got into a row with the Chief Forester about the punishing of small mills for waste, yet letting the two larger mills get away with an equal amount simply by giving their waste a different designation. The matter came to a head when one day he was sent from Burns Lake to a site about forty miles in the bush and told to measure and fine a small mill for over-sized slabs. He had already seen and reported a huge pile of even larger over-sized slabs in the big local mill and been told to "mind his own business." Upon bringing this to the Chief Forester's attention, he was again told it was none of his affair, his duty was to do as ordered—fine the small mill. When telling the story later, Trevor said with a chuckle, "Wonder of wonders, the small mill burned their slab-pile so there was no evidence. Wonder who tipped them off. . ." Needless to say, he "caught hell" as he said, and no doubt if he hadn't quit on the spot, he would have been fired. So Trevor happily returned to Masset Inlet, although it did mean looking for a new job.

With his office experience he had little difficulty in securing work as a time-keeper at Camp Number 3 in Juskatla Inlet, then later worked in Buckley Bay as a lumber-grader until the mill shut down in the mid-1920s.

From there on it was catch-as-catch-can as he went the gamut of jobs, first having a try as a small logging camp operator for a few years, when with a small crew of men working for him, he took out logs from land he bought near the north end of Kumdis Slough. Disappearing markets made that totally unprofitable. Later, for a few years, he did a stint as postmaster, using the former office of Cooper Young as the post office. As soon as the government changed, the job went to a supporter of the new government, a common situation in that era. He also had several summer sessions as a Federal Fisheries officer, as well as taking his stint at the bottom of the Depression doing the road work the government meted out to men in need for top pay of $3.00 a day. This work was usually limited to three days a month per man. Like all his neighbours he had much difficulty in making ends meet. By 1930 the mills, logging camps, mining operations, and surveying contracts which had previously provided the job opportunities for the Masset Inlet men succumbed to the Depression and closed down. Except for the Baxter Pole Camp.

In 1928 the J.H. Baxter Company, a California based operation with an office in Vancouver, British Columbia, had begun a project at Ferguson Bay to log cedar poles. They built a camp and hired pole-cutters, plus the usual back-up crew to get the poles out to tide-water for transport to market by big log-carrying ships owned by the Baxter Company. They logged the poles for two years at Ferguson Bay, then moved operations to Mayer Lake for another two years, after which the camp and equipment went to the east side of Kumdis Island, about two miles from the south entrance to Kumdis Slough.

Trevor didn't work for the Baxter Company, but his son John did during the time the camp was at Mayer Lake from 1930 to 1931. John and his pal, Charlie Minaker, who lived near the Kumdis Bridge, were taken on and felt fortunate to have a job in those lean years. But the work was rigorous and hours long, and the living conditions not the best. The camp had been built too close to the lake, which of course rose several feet in the heavy rains of fall. The bunkhouse floors were flooded, and the wash house and outside privies were similarly inundated. The water did not subside for several weeks. As the flimsy walls of the bunkhouses were inadequate for winter weather the places were always cold. However, despite living conditions and constantly aching muscles, the work was interesting.

Baxters demanded that their cedar poles be arrow-straight with absolutely no defects, and the actual pole-cutting was done on a piece-work basis. Initially each polemaker was paid less than two cents a foot, but by the spring of 1929, before the camp left Ferguson Bay, this had been raised to three cents. Not only did the pole-cutter have to fall each tree so that no damage occurred during the operation, but he also had to limb it, then peel all the bark off. By hand. Each pole-cutter was assigned an area by the cruiser, and he would have to satisfy this man that he had taken all the merchantable poles from it before he was given another section.

The poles would then be cold-decked ready for removal to tide-water. Getting the poles into a cold-deck pile was accomplished by using a small one-cylinder yarder, and instead of chokers, a cone-shaped bell was attached to the end of the pole to be pulled. In all three operations, Ferguson Bay, Mayer Lake, and on Kumdis Island, the Baxter Company utilized a unique wooden railroad to transport the poles from the forest to tide-water, where they were towed out to the waiting ship.

The wooden railroad consisted of eight-inch hemlock logs, laid end-to-end, similar to rails on a train-track. Special custom-built Fordson tractors, three in all, each with a detachable trailer, were ordered from the Westminster Iron Works. These tractors and trailers were all equipped with big twelve-inch flange wheels, and a special drive ratio enabling the tractors to reach a top speed of twenty miles per hour, ahead or in reverse. They had no steering wheel—guidance was by the brake wheel. Started on gasoline, they ran on distillate—an inexpensive, crude type of kerosene which had a vile smell. Although dubbed Tugaways when manufactured, the tractor units were never called this by the men who knew them. They gave them the curious name of "humdergins," or else referred to them simply as the "pole tractors."

There was a two-mile pole railroad at Ferguson Bay, a four-mile one into Mayer Lake, and another two-mile one on Kumdis Island, which went from the edge of Kumdis Slough into the Kumdis Lake area in the centre of the island. The Mayer Lake railroad went from the head of Kumdis Bay and for much of its route followed the old wagon road which had been built for settlers on preemptions at Loon Lake and Mayer Lake between 1911 and 1920. A few of the married men who worked for the Mayer Lake operation lived in some of those old homesites at Mayer Lake.

By the time operations wound up in 1933 on Kumdis Island, only two of the old pole tractors were in working condition,

The bunk-house area of the J.H. Baxter Pole Company's Mayer Lake operation.

In rainy season when the lake rose, water would cover the floors of the lower lying bunk-houses. Man in photo is Frank Appleby, the bull-cook who kept the place supplied with firewood.

Photo–J.H. Baxter Co.

In 1928 the J.H. Baxter Pole Company brought three of these uniquely-designed Fordson tractors to haul their poles from the forests of Graham Island to tide-water. Officially designed as Tugaways, the men who worked with them never used this term. They referred to them either as the pole tractors or, more commonly, the "humdergins." The remains of the machine above is in the Port Clements Museum today.

The pole road to Mayer Lake, along which the Tugaways ran. The Baxter Company also had similar roads at thei Ferguson Bay and Kumdis Island operation.

Both photos—J.H. Baxter Company

the third machine being used just for parts. There were still twenty thousand poles to be cut, but market conditions had deteriorated drastically, and Baxter Company records show that they were only able to sell a mere 270 poles that year. (In contrast to a few years later, in 1942, when fifty-nine thousand poles were sold.)

In addition to the main camp, Baxters also had several small gyppo camps getting out poles for them—among which was one operated by members of the Pelton family, who lived on Kumdis Island, close to the Baxter camp. When Baxters closed down in 1933, they put everything up for sale at bargain prices, and included among the items were the unique pole tractors. Asking price was $100.00 for the two in working condition, plus any parts which remained from the third. Two of the Pelton brothers, Alfred and Ralph, together with their brother-in-law, Jack Hewison, persuaded two other neighbours, Frank Pozan and Stanley Mowling, to form a group and buy the machines with a view to harvesting the remaining twenty thousand poles when markets improved. But their dream was not to be—conditions grew steadily worse, and a second world war put the final finish to the idea.

Although it took some searching, jobs of one sort or another were available for younger men, such as John Williams, Charlie Minaker, and the two Pelton brothers. The Southeaster Mine near Skidegate was hiring a few labourers; the large logging camps of J.R. Morgan, T.A. Kelley, and A.P. Allison on Moresby Island and in Skidegate Inlet also took a few with good strong backs. And there was always trolling on the fishing grounds off Langara Island in a gas boat. For those too strapped to buy even an old clunker of a boat, an open skiff was utilized to fish.

For older men, however, jobs were almost non-existent. As mentioned earlier, Trevor had to do his stint for while on the government road projects and found work as a Federal Fisheries officer for a few summers plus occasional remuneration as a Notary Public and Justice of the Peace. But by 1933 he had to make a hard decision about his beloved homesite.

With money in such short supply he couldn't afford to pay taxes on land other than the property actually needed to live on. Much as he hated living in the centre of any town, it was obvious that this was where he would have to be for several more years. Both his daughters were still in school—Betty taking high school by correspondence with the assistance of the teacher and Nancy in grade five. As he agonized over a solution to his dilemma he had a visitor. Dave Tuft, now well on in years, wanted to move closer to town. The five-mile hike into his Skid Road homesite with a heavy pack of groceries was proving too taxing for his frail figure, and the alternative of a thirty-mile trip in an open boat to his other home on Striae Island had also become too difficult.

"I was wondering about that cabin John McDougall built on your old preemption, T.L." Dave began. "The one up on the ridge beside the two Jims. Took a look at it the other day, and it's still in fair shape. I talked to Mac about it, and he says he hasn't used it in years—not since he built his house here in Port. Anyhow, he doesn't want it, but since he never owned the land it's on, he figures by rights it belongs to you. So how do you feel? Would you consider selling it to me?"

"Oh, for heavens sakes, Dave," was the reply. "Go and live in it anytime you want, man. You are more than welcome as far as I'm concerned. You most certainly don't have to buy it!"

"No," said Mr. Tuft. "I know you mean well, but I don't like being beholden to anyone—like to be my own man. I have a small annuity, so there's a few dollars to spare. You don't have to worry about that aspect. I'd really feel better if I bought it . . ."

Trevor leaned back in his chair and looked at the older man carefully. He knew that were he in Tuft's shoes he, too, would want to be his own man, but in this case there was a problem.

"Trouble is, Dave," he confided. "I'm in quite a quandry about that whole place at this time. There's about $100 due on it in taxes, and I just don't know how I'm going to handle it now that work is so scarce. It seems to need all I earn to take care of family expenses. Can't make up my mind what to do."

The two men sat in silence for a few minutes, then Trevor had an inspiration. "Tell you what. You pay the hundred dollars and take over the whole place. I'd a damsite rather it went to you than the ruddy government—and its only a question of time before that will happen, I'm afraid."

"The whole preemption for a hundred dollars, T.L.—that's ridiculous! I expected to pay that for the cabin alone. No, no, no...I couldn't possibly accept such an offer."

"God knows I hate to part with the place," Trevor had to admit. "But sooner or later I am going to lose it the way things are going. If I have to let it go for taxes, lord-only-knows-who might end up with it. At least with you I know I'd have someone there with an appreciation of things. Look, I tell you what, Dave—how about you taking it over now, and if in years to come it seems feasible for Meta and I to go back there to live, well you can sell us the waterfront part where our cabin is for a nominal fee. What would you think of that?"

Mr. Tuft shook his head dubiously. However, there followed more persuasion by Trevor, and at last he said, "Well, alright. I don't want the waterfront part in any case. I like it back up in the woods—trail runs right past Bill Vyse's—I can drop in on him when I go to town. You can have the beach part whenever you say. Okay. Go ahead...make out the papers. Its a deal."

In 1933 a new baby was born into the Williams family—the first grandchild for Meta and Trevor. Son John had married his childhood sweetheart, Doreen Dunn of Masset, the year before, and their daughter, Jean Mary, was born in Masset, not too far from the little house her father had first seen the light of day in and where Mrs. Millard had introduced him to a taste of rum in his nightly bottle "to settle him down." Jean was a bonny child and a daily joy to her grandparents. Two years later a second grandchild, James Cecil, arrived to be also welcomed and greatly fussed over.

Times might have been hard, and money in short supply, but as is usually the case when people are thrown on their own resources, a great community feeling existed. Card parties, dances, impromptu concerts, and picnics were the order of the day. Of course many of the older people in the community had been together through the early pioneer days and had a good understanding of this sort of life so fell into the swing of things with ease. Every family had a productive vegetable garden, and fish and game were still plentiful for the table, and

although diets might become monotonous during the winter
months, no one needed to go hungry. It was perhaps as good a
place as any to weather out a depression, even one of this
magnitude.

Dave Tuft moved into the old McDougall cabin, and being
only a mile from the outskirts of Port Clements, felt as though
he was really in town, so he told the Williams', whom he visited
frequently to report on "the place." Trevor never regretted for
an instant his deal with this old friend of theirs, and apparently
Mr. Tuft was equally happy with the arrangement.

An avid reader and philosopher, one of Dave Tufts's pet
topics was the coming of technocracy. A great favourite with
several youngsters in their early teens, he would expound on
the subject at some length to his young visitors, who didn't
always comprehend the wisdom of his words. They were more
interested in the tasty meal he would serve up—invariably
potatoes, onions, and bacon fried in a skillet on top of his
wood-fired heater in the ex-McDougall cabin. A large skylight
provided most of the light in the one-room place.

Trevor's daughter, Betty, was among those who regularly
visited the elderly man and could long remember his admonition. "You should take this seriously. It will be your generation
that will have to rearrange their lives as machines take over
from men. One machine will replace fifty men—perhaps
more. Machines will be more important than men." But the
whole idea seemed so improbable to the young people listening to him—young people who in the early 1930s were used to
doing everything by hand—their drinking water was hauled by
a bucket from a well, wood-chopping an expected chore, and
so on. All this talk of machines and what they would be doing
was beyond belief. They respected the old man's words but
were not alarmed by them. Today, however, they recall those
sessions with him around his stove in that small cabin in the
woods and realize everything he told them has ultimately proved to be as he predicted.

SEVENTEEN

AS THE PROSPERITY OF the early 1920s changed into the economic disaster of the 1930s, people who had swarmed into the Masset Inlet area to take advantage of work and good pay in the logging and lumbering activities just as quickly left again hoping for better opportunities elsewhere. The mills in Port Clements had closed, never to reopen—except for a couple of sporadic ventures on the old Barton site. H.R. Beaven of Queen Charlotte City had a small tie and timber project there from 1929 to 1932, then Malcolm Milloy took over the site and operated his shingle and lumber mill in 1933—both very small businesses employing few men.

The big mill at Buckley Bay shipped its last load of lumber in October 1924, and closed down completely in April, 1925. A watchman and one or two families stayed on for a few years, then the houses were sold at give-away prices. For instance, a five-roomed house could be purchased for $30. The buyer had only to jack it down the hill onto a raft, and it was his. Within a few years little was left of this once-booming mill-town. In neighbouring Sewall the busy mill owned and operated by the Vancouver Trading Company had closed down, and by the 1930s only two families remained, Julius and Hilde Grewe and their son, Willie, and Mr. and Mrs. Paul Bastian with their son and daughter, Paul Jr. and Frieda.

All the main logging camps around the area had closed, save for one or two gyppo (small owner-operated) camps, which opened for brief periods now and then to supply a small sawmill run at Masset by Arthur Robertson. Even the Baxter Pole camps were closed after 1933. Port Clements dwindled to little more than eighty people. Those who elected to stay sensed they could be in for a long haul in belt-tightening, "But it will be the same everywhere," they told one another. "At least here everybody owns the place they are on, so there are no landlords to worry about. Also, in a small place neighbours keep an eye out for anyone having trouble." And it would be possible to barter to offset lack of cash—labour in exchange for material, a cake for a nice wild goose, or one type of labour traded for another, such as laundry in exchange for digging a garden.

With so many ex-loggers now part of the community and unable to indulge in their customary "sprees" in lower mainland cities, it was inevitable that experiments in home brew were soon underway. And there were few homes which did not follow suit—the beverages ranging from the vinegars of the unsuccessful attempts to the ginger and malt beers, wines, and the more potent "moonshine" needing the familiar still and mash to concoct. This latter product, manufactured by those hoping to commercialize their efforts, was conducted on the quiet, until the tell-tale yeasty odour of a brew being run-off gave the show away. Yet it was comparatively rare to see drunkenness in public, other than some high spirits at a dance as the evening wore on.

Bill Hastie's dance hall and poolroom burned to the ground in the early 1930s, along with his residence and bakery, but with the shrinking population it was not missed as greatly as might have been the case a few years earlier. The Hasties left soon after the fire, moving to Masset where Bill ran a small bakery for a few years. His excellent bread found a ready market. The community hall, built by invitation from the minister on property adjacent to St. Mark's Anglican Church, became the main centre for village activities, supplemented

The town might be small, but there was always plenty going on. This is the July 1st, 1927 picnic held (as always) in the grassy field beside Bert Tingley's hotel.

St. Mark's Church drew a fair congregation for the afternoon services held every other Sunday. Building left of centre is the first community hall. Photo taken in 1927.

Port Clements in the 1930s. Photo taken from the deck of the *Prince John*, as she tied to the dock. Light-coloured rooftop on the left is the former GWVA building. Ruins of the old Lewis mill on the shore between GWVA and the dock. Large building on right of dock is the beer parlour—note beer barrels on dock waiting to be shipped out. They contain empty bottles packed in straw. The leaning tree in the centre was a cedar, topped and limbed, used as a wireless mast previously. Photo is from a postcard.

Second tennis court in Port Clements was built of wood planks, and was a fast court. Very popular with adults and children.
Photo–Mrs. Edith Dyson

Mr. and Mrs. L. Dyson. Edith Dyson and Meta Williams were long-time friends, who shared a cup of tea twice a week for some thirty-five years.
Photo—Mrs. L. Dyson

Port Clements—1936. Tennis court is visible in upper right. Lynch Mill in lower right, showing signs of decay. Bare patch on left of wharf is site of Lewis Mill. The ex-GWVA is first large building along the road to the left, with the Tingley Hotel in the field beyond it. Photo taken a low tide shows how shallow Stewart Bay is.
Photo—G.S. Andrew

September, 1943—the wedding of their younger daughter Nancy. *Left to right*: Albert and Betty Dalzell, best man Audie Mattson, Meta and Trevor Williams, Len and Nancy Orr, Mr. and Mrs. Orr, Sr. and Mary Dyson, bridesmaid. Photo taken in the front garden of the Williams' new home.

Looking west. The view of Masset Inlet is the same today as it was when Trevor first saw it. The entrance to Juskatla Inlet is on the left, where the dark point stretches into the Inlet.

occasionally by the dining room in the Tingley Hotel.

The Tingleys had left Port Clements in the mid-1920s, deciding they had weathered enough storms in the community and it was time to try an easier life-style in their home town of Victoria. However, the key for the hotel was left with Bill Rennie, who had permission to open the dining room for dances and entertainments as needed. The town's hotel needs were met in part by Frank Pearce's rooms upstairs in the ex-GWVA building, as well as the rooms upstairs in the building built by Frank Hicks during the war as a poolroom-hotel, near the approach to the government wharf. This hotel was purchased in the late 1920s by a trio consisting of Herb Hampton, Jimmy Ciccone, and another man who only stayed briefly. The Hamptons and Ciccones, well liked in the village, remained until the early 1930s, taking part in all community activities. Their hotel was probably only viable because of the beer parlour installed when they took over. It was the first such establishment on the Charlottes.

The large, grassy acre of land which Bert Tingley had cleared on the east side of his hotel was in constant use as a ball-field and picnic site and especially came into its own on July 1st each year when the entire community turned out for the races and other activities held there. The old hotel kitchen, with its long counters and tables, would be opened for the hard-working committee to set out the big bowls of salads, desserts, hot drinks, and other picnic foods provided by the women of the community. The dining room also served as a place to eat in case of inclement weather on that special day—something all experienced Islanders know has to be kept in mind when planning any festivities. In appreciation of its connection with this annual celebration, the field was commonly called "The July Field" by all Port residents for many years.

The wooden tennis-court built on the hill west of the school had steady use, adults and youngsters making the trek up the hill for daily games whenever weather permitted. This tennis court had been built during the 1914–18 war years after the slab-pile from Barton's mill had obliterated the earlier clay one. Spearheading the drive for the second court was David

Maxwell, "Maxie," formerly of the Centre Meridian homesteaders. Maxie had been a Davis Cup winner in his native
Ontario, and his patient coaching helped more than a few
novices become reasonably adept. Meta and Trevor Williams
were among the regular patrons of the court, and Meta
especially loved the game, taking part in the tournaments
until she was in her mid-fifties. Her underhand serve
contrasted markedly with the overhand style which supersed-
ed it and was in common use by this time. But she made her
points just as skillfully using the old-fashioned method she had
learned as a girl in Swansea.

In 1924, a few years after he had purchased the ex-Cooper
Young house on the hill in Port Clements, Trevor had also
bought a two-and-half acre strip of waterfront on the edge of
the townsite, near the mouth of the Yakoun River—the price
being an irresistible $24. It was heavily treed, and he planned
to use it as a woodlot, falling the trees into the water and
rafting them round to a beach-site closer to the house on the
hill. Then he would hire Bill Rennie and his team of horses to
haul the logs up the hill to be cut into blocks for his family's
fuel supply. And with each session he would lament the
inconvenience and cost of the operation. "If only we lived
closer to the water..."

In the late 1930s their tennis-playing friend, Maxie, bought
several acres which adjoined Trevor's woodlot, and in clearing
his garden spot Maxie discovered he had excellent gravel on
his place. He was able to interest the Department of Highways
in this, and they subsequently built a road into the site to
enable their trucks to haul the gravel out as needed. As the
road ran along the top edge of Trevor's property, it was the
break he was looking for to leave the detested house on the hill
(detested only by Trevor—Meta had always enjoyed living
there). Adding to his desire to be rid of the place was the fact
that the highways department had substantially upgraded the
road leading to the hated house, and the government had
tripled the taxes of all those who lived along it.

By this time both he and Meta realized they would never
return to the preemption, but Trevor thought the woodlot
location would be almost as good. It was on waterfront, had a

magnificent view south and west, privacy, good garden soil, modest taxes, and now the much-needed road access. Meta, who like Trevor was approaching her sixtieth year, was not so sure about the advantages of moving out to live in the bush again. "There are bears on that road," she told him. "I'll be scared to death every time I want to come in to the store. And who would want to come to see us if they have to walk that last half mile wondering if they'll run into one of the beasts?"

But Trevor managed to dispel her anxiety, pointing out that there would be trucks in and out to the gravel pit, as well as visitors to Maxie's, and promising to walk with her every time she went out along the section she worried about. "I am quite sure that once we are using the road on a regular basis the bears will leave," he told her. "They don't hang around populated places for long." Then he sugared the idea a bit more by pointing out the numerous defects of their present home and describing how it would possible to avoid such annoyances in designing a future home.

They had both always admired the two-story frame house built by Sid Wormald for Charlie Adam in Graham Centre in 1913. Adam had sold it to Felix Graham, who had lived in it with his wife and son until he went overseas in 1916. Graham had returned to live for a few months after the war, then abandoned the place and left for good. There was a hole in the roof where shingles had blown off, but fortunately the house had suffered little in the way of vandalism. When Trevor decided to venture into the logging business in the mid-1920s, he bought the place from Graham for $50 and fixed it up as a cook-house and dining room, with two bunk rooms upstairs. Taking it on a raft through Kumdis Slough, he moved it to his property near the north end of Kumdis Island. When the logging operation came to an end due to non-existent markets, he had the house and raft towed into Port Clements and beached on the grassy area east of the old Barton mill site. Son John, and his wife, Doreen, lived in the place for a few years until they found more suitable quarters. Trevor had been eyeing this house, still in excellent condition, as he mulled over the notion of moving to his Yakoun woodlot.

He drew various plans for remodelling the place and, as he

showed them to Meta for her suggestions, explained that he had found an excellent source of water on the Yakoun property. "We can easily have running water," he told her. (This was the ultimate luxury at that time.) "I'll do like Bert Tingley, put in an elevated tank and pump it full each day—or more if we need it. There's lots of water in that stream—even in the middle of summer. Not like the well at this place. Draw more than a few buckets, and we have problems in the dry periods." Then one more enticement. "I'm thinking of a small lighting plant. What would you say to a few electric lights? Nice change from the oil lamps we use now?"

Meta shook her head and patted his hand lovingly, "How can I resist? It sounds marvellous!" However, she added, "But Trevor, what a job moving all our household things will be. I dread the thought of living using bits and pieces and transferring the rest, trying to guess what we'll need each day. I suppose I'm getting old, but really, the prospect is quite daunting."

Luck was on Trevor's side. Storekeeper Frank Pearce wanted to take an extended holiday in California about that time. He needed someone to operate the store during his absence and also had to have the building continuously occupied to fulfill insurance requirements. He put the idea to the Williams.' "I'll be gone about ten months," he said. "How about living in my place while you make your move? I realize you'll be too busy getting the new house ready to think about running the store as well, but what about Betty? I could show her the ropes in a week. . .not really all that much to it. Do you think she would be interested?"

It was an ideal solution. Trevor and Meta could work at renovating their Yakoun house then move their furniture at leisure. Betty, now nineteen and recently back from taking a business course in Prince Rupert, certainly needed that type of work experience in the worst way, and Meta, an expert accountant, could keep a close eye on things. Nancy was still in school, taking her grade ten by correspondence with assistance from the teacher (a subsidy was paid to the teacher by the parents of pupils requiring this help).

Bringing in the small donkey-engine he had used in his

logging operation, Trevor set about clearing a large area for garden and house on the Yakoun property. The ex-Graham Centre house was towed to the site, hauled up on skids, and remodelled. By the time Frank Pearce returned from his holiday in May of 1939, all was in readiness for the Williams family to begin living in their new location.

The unlamented house on the hill was abandoned to the tax man. It was acquired in the next tax sale by the Roman Catholic Church, used as a place of worship for some years, then latterly as a residence for two of that church's parishioners, Cecile and Helen Dunroe. They were the unmarried daughters of the irascible Frank Lennie le Tonturier Donroe, the man Mrs. Rowan had tried so hard to persuade Charlie Adam to give a "wee bitty land" to so that Graham Centre might have at least a temporary school. (Over the years the name Donroe had become commonly known as Dunroe.) By the time Helen and Cecile moved into Port Clements, their parents and older brothers were dead, and other members of the large family had left the area, and these two had to fend for themselves. Both women were partially handicapped, having had polio in infancy. But they were able to look after themselves as long as they had a helping hand with heavier chores, such as wood and so on. Cecile even precariously drove an decrepit Model A truck.

The newly-renovated house the Williams' moved to was very comfortable, much more livable than the one they had left. And as Trevor had predicted, with the increase in traffic on the road fronting their place, bears soon left the area for good and were rarely, if ever seen. But to be on the safe side for the first while, Trevor made sure he walked with Meta along the section of the road she worried about, then went to meet her when she returned. Neighbours who had visited them in their former house on the hill also came to see them in their new location. Among the visitors was Meta's long-time friend, Edith Dyson, who lived at the far end of the town—nearly a mile from this new house. Mrs. Dyson and Meta met twice a week, for over thirty years. On Tuesdays, at 2 p.m., Meta would go for tea at the Dysons, and on Fridays at 2 p.m., Edith Dyson would arrive at Meta's for tea. For all those years these two proper British ladies never called each other by anything but their formal married names, Mrs. Dyson and Mrs. Williams, yet they were firm and devoted friends. However, this was true for the most part of all women of that era—first names were seldom, if ever, used.

Life had settled into a pleasant routine by the summer of 1939, but changes were already under way. With work so scarce on the Charlottes, especially for girls, the older ones left to seek jobs on the mainland. This was also true in the Williams family. Betty left in June of that year, and Nancy followed in August. Meta and Trevor were on their own for the first time in years.

On September 3rd, 1939, came the news that another World War had begun in Europe. It seemed unbelievable.

"Well, I can't shoulder a gun in the trenches any more," Trevor told Meta, "but I wouldn't feel comfortable if I didn't offer my services in some capacity. At least I do know army life and the organization that has to exist in setting things up. God knows I hate the thought of getting stuck behind a desk. But perhaps I could be of help in that end of things somewhere or other."

He was fifty-nine at the time, and for years rigorously exercised for an hour every morning before breakfast, a routine which included not only the customary push-ups and so on, but also a work-out on a trapeze which hung from the roof inside his spacious woodshed. The work-outs gave him no problems whatsoever. A recent medical had shown that his heart, blood-pressure, and other vital signs were in first-class condition, so he expected to breeze through any physical exam the enlistment office would put him through.

But he was rejected immediately when he underwent the army medical. "Varicose veins," he was told. "Varicose veins!" he snorted. "What on earth difference could they make to someone in an office chair? Or even going on the double from one place to another. As you can plainly see I'm in excellent health. I am past the days of active trench combat, but I surely could be of service doing pencil-work. My record in the last war should certainly prove that I've had a fair bit of experience in the administrative end of things as well as combat duty. You

are going to need men with this sort of background—
particularly at this organizational stage."

However, the medical rejection stood. The examining board
would not be swayed otherwise. And besides, they told him,
he really was over-age at forty-five—the age he had given
them for this first session. He planned to deal with the age
discrepancy once he had been accepted, never dreaming it
would be varicose veins they would zero in on. "I don't think
they'll be so fussy later on," he told Meta when he returned
from the mainland, "because this war has all the indications of
a long haul. Well, at least I've offered my help."

Although she had realized Trevor would doubtless be put in
a desk job had he been accepted, nevertheless it was an
infinite relief for Meta to have the matter decided as it had
been. But although they would be far from the actual horrors
of this war, and Trevor was safe by her side, the hostilities
would still take a heavy emotional toll. Her nephews would be
killed, one in the Hong Kong disaster, others in the sinking of
the *Hood*, and in the battles over London. News of the
bombings of her people in Britain, especially the four-day blitz
of Swansea, was agonizing. It was equally bad for Trevor's
family. His younger brother, Graham, and his wife not only
lost both their sons but were themselves bombed out
twice—escaping in their night-clothes during air-attacks on
London. Anxiety over the constant peril their relations were
under reactivated the vivid and painful memories of World
War One when Trevor was in danger. Added to this was
concern about Betty.

Shortly after the war had broken out this daughter had been
stricken with tuberculosis—a killer disease at that time. She
was gravely ill for months and her recovery uncertain. But
after a long wait for a bed in the over-crowded sanitariums of
that day, she finally underwent treatment which turned the
tide and, over a three-year period, did regain her health. Meta
had been quite shattered by the news and terribly frustrated at
being so far from her daughter during her illness. The strain of
it all became unbearable. Today it would be called "burn-out."
By the time Betty returned home in July 1942, Meta's health
had deteriorated noticeably.

But the bright spot that month was Betty's wedding to Albert Dalzell, a young Prince Rupert shipwright she had met shortly before she became ill, and who had courted her all through the three years of recovery. Her parents were thrilled when she chose their cosy living room for the ceremony. The following year Nancy married Len Orr, who worked in nearby Juskatla as a log scaler. This daughter was also married in her parents' home, much to their delight. The Dalzells returned to Prince Rupert to live, but Nancy and her husband remained on the Charlottes for several years and visited Meta and Trevor frequently. More grandchildren were born. Eight in all—two sons and a daughter for Betty and five daughters for Nancy.

Although the war took many of the sons of their British relations, by a strange and happy quirk this was not to be the case in their immediate family. Son John, upon appearing before the medical examining office to enlist for war service, was rejected oddly enough for the same reason as Trevor— varicose veins. And both sons-in-law were also turned down for medical reasons. So at least Meta and Trevor were spared the pain of their own family being in active combat.

Actually the second World War was not nearly as devastating for the men of the Queen Charlottes as had been the case in the 1914–18 war. The main reason was that quite a number could not pass the medicals. Many were rejected as physically unfit, which no doubt says something about the effect on young bodies of the Great Depression which preceded this second world conflict.

The end of the war in 1945 meant relief in the worry load about overseas relations. Now the news from Britain was about more normal happenings, enabling Meta and Trevor to relax and pursue their daily activities with a sense of future. Only Nancy and her husband and daughters were still on the Queen Charlottes by then. Betty and Albert lived in Prince Rupert, and John with his wife and family were in Ocean Falls. Later, in the 1950s, Nancy and family also moved to the mainland.

Trevor and Meta were kept busy with their bountiful garden, bridge games, and various community activities. Meta continued to play the small foot-pumped organ for the services at St. Mark's and taught some of the Sunday School classes. Trips off Islands were undertaken to visit their children, especially at Christmas, when each of the families would be visited for several weeks in turn. Then in the summer months, the grandchildren were brought by their parents to see Trevor and Meta.

But Meta's health steadily worsened, and despite every care and constant medical help, she grew more frail each year. By July 1st, 1958, she was so weak Trevor was advised to take her to the small hospital in Queen Charlotte City. With much tenderness their kind neighbours helped him make her as comfortable as possible for the forty-five-mile trip in a taxi. Six days later, on July 7th, she passed away.

It was a grievous loss for Trevor. He was now seventy-eight and for sixty-three of those years his very existence had been motivated by his love for this woman—first as childhood sweethearts, then as young adults, and finally as man and wife. His daughters came to help in the first weeks of the grief, Nancy wisely bringing with her his newest grandchild, a bubbly six-month girl, whose gurgles and smiles cheered everyone.

Son John, who had lost his own wife a few years earlier, came when the girls left, and father and son shared many memories of early years to further ease the terrible loss. Gradually, in the peace and beauty of this beloved island he had chosen to live on, the joy of the outdoors and the work which had to be accomplished each day—wood-cutting, gardening, and domestic chores—the healing process began, and he was able to face his changed circumstances and build a semblance of worth into his life.

About three years after Meta's death, daughter Betty began to compile a comprehensive history of the Charlottes and begged for his help. The diaries of his early years were dug out, and he laboriously translated the shorthand he had used into the longhand she needed for her notes. He was tireless in his patient research, not only into his own memories, but in looking up other oldsters who would add to the information. The project went on for five years for one book and then another five years for a second volume. His contributions were of inestimable value.

Bridge games were always a continuing highlight of his enjoyment, and he would drop everything to take part in a game, night or day. He was an excellent player—although he could be rash in his bidding. It was not unknown for him, when he had a partner whom he felt was unduly timid about the value of her (or his) hand, to promptly bid what he thought probably more properly reflected the situation. This led to some problems when his hunches were incorrect, but he could usually charm his way out of the indignation directed at his brashness.

Winter months, especially the long evenings with no one to talk to at home, began to weigh heavily on Trevor, so he became a traveller for those periods. One of his first trips was to Jamaica and the Grand Cayman Islands, where he bicycled around the area in shorts in his eighty-third year. Next year he flew to Hawaii with his old pioneering friend, Charlie Adam, and Charlie's wife, Suzie, to stay in a rented home for a month. With three children, ten grandchildren, and a growing number of great-grandchildren, he was off to visit most of them in their various homes around British Columbia each winter—and on one occasion went as far east as Ottawa to stay with one granddaughter. While there he was invited to lunch with the local MP (at that time Frank Howard), and watched the antics in the House. He was impressed with Prime Minister Trudeau's mental agility as he took on Robert Stanfield and David Lewis, "Both very decent, honourable men, but nowhere near Trudeau when it came to debating. It was a joy to watch the man."

In 1972 when the CBC decided to do a documentary about life on the Queen Charlotte Islands, Trevor and another old-timer, Charlie Hartie of Queen Charlotte City, along with a later arrival, Howard Phillips of Masset, were asked to be part of one scene. They were requested to come to a Queen Charlotte City cafe, sit at a table and reminisce, then as the "Take One" was called the three men were told, "Please be funny."

The directive must have been successfully carried out as in

1974 the producer, Mike Poole, arranged to do another documentary, this time featuring Trevor's early life and memories. After extensive preparations the crew were due to arrive in July of that year to begin filming. But the week before they came Trevor suffered a massive stroke which affected his speech and ability to walk. He was ninety-four.

Up to the day of his illness he had been completely mobile and active, even to riding his bicycle, doing his daily push-ups, and keeping his sizeable garden in excellent shape. It had been a good life and an interesting one. For the next two years, however, it was necessary for him to enter first the local Queen Charlotte hospital, then transfer to extended care in Prince Rupert. He was not a good patient, nor an adaptable one. He fought routine from beginning to end, ignoring any rules that he found foolish to his way of thinking.

But it was during these latter two years that he again helped with a book, for it was at this time that I began to question him regarding his war years and more details of his early life with my mother. He patiently dug back into his memories again and saw to it that I obtained as much information as possible from old papers and letters to supplement his own recollections and diaries, so that at a later time I could write this book—although I am sure he didn't dream that he would be the central character.

Trevor died on September 8th, 1976, aged ninety-six, and was buried beside his Meta in the peaceful Tlell cemetery where many of their friends and neighbours also lie.

INDEX

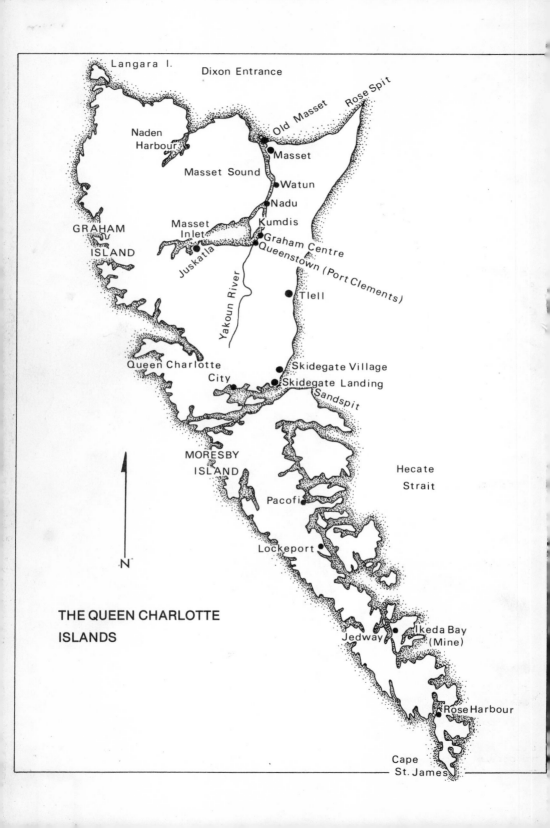

THE QUEEN CHARLOTTE
ISLANDS